* Victoria Rey *

Magical Seals

Ancient Secrets of Amulets, Charms, Symbols, & Talismans

Plus DIY Instructions on How to Make Your Own Magical Seals.

© All rights reserved. No part of this book may be reproduced in text or images by any means, without written permission.

© 1st Edition Calli Casa Editorial 2023

Yhacar Trust, 2023

By VICTORIA REY

General Supervision: Bernabé Pérez.

www.2GoodLuck.com

Calli Casa Editorial

Lake Elsinore, CA 92530

Magical Seals... what are they anyway?

Talismans, seals, charms, or fetishes are usually portable objects made of different materials, associated with magical or religious beliefs. They are intended to protect, heal, or even harm individuals.

From formal to folk traditions, through the ages and across many civilizations, these talismans can be traced upon from ancient to modern times. You will find here symbols from Eastern and Western astrological, scientific, and religious practices.

These symbols can be reproduced on metal, wood, fabric, leather, parchment, etcetera. They are charged with energy and astral forces by the person who prepares them.

They can be copied to be concealed within clothes, books, hidden spots on houses or businesses, or can be openly displayed for all to see.

They can be prayed upon, used in rituals, or for spell casting.

Many of them are intended to better the life of the possessor. For example, they may see improvement in their endeavors while hunting, fishing, homesteading, trading, or with money transactions in general. Speaking of money, you will find plenty of seals and talismans on this book intended for the possessor to gain riches, power, and social statuses as well.

Other seals are used to heal their own bodies or minds or those of their beloved ones.

But the most common use of these symbols is for protection. They have been used time and again, while in war or at peace, while at home or traveling, and also when taking risky actions. Protection seals, talismans, or amulets have been carried to protect the possessor, their family and friends, as well as their properties.

A few of the seals you will find within this book are also used to control others, which brings us to the dark side of the seals: black magic. When a sorcerer uses these symbols to control or harm others, they are bringing dark energy into the lives of those who are meant to receive harm, as well as the sorcerer who is casting that harm. Be mindful if you use them for these purposes because if you don't know how to control dark forces, they are better left alone.

Some sorcerers use lengthy conjurations or special rituals before using these seals, while others only use a set of magical words or a simple prayer. It all depends on their preferences, or the type of magic they are performing.

How to Use Magical Seals

To use these seals you have to have a particular goal.

Then go ahead and choose the seal you are going to use.

Once defined, you can choose what type of material you want to use to reproduce the seal.

Also, you need to define if you will carry it with you, hide it, or display it.

This will determine the size and material you will use.

When you are ready to use your seal, you will need to determine how you will charge it with your energy.

You can perform a ritual in front of your altar, if you have one, go to a temple of your preference or a quiet space where you feel confortable to consecrate your seal for the purposes you need it.

Firstly, decide if you want to go with a conjuration or with a simple prayer. Then, state the purpose of your seal with your own words. For example,

I consecrate this seal to protect me and my loved ones.... or I consecrate this seal to bring in prosperity to my business (state name).

After that, say the conjuration and/or the prayer of your choice, or both if so you decide.

You can use one of the prayers in the next chapter, or simply write on your own words of love, thankfulness, and petition to your Higher Power. In some Pagan religions they write words in a poem format that can be read following the beat of a drum.

You can use oils, perfumes, candles, salt, incense, or holy water to consecrate your space and your seal.

Bottom line: there is no right or wrong. This is your seal, this is your ritual, this is you calling the shots. Tools and ingredients are to aid your focus on your petition.

<u>The only thing really important while performing magic is that your energy, thoughts, and words are vibrating high to reach the frequency of your petition. If you can keep all of them, before, on, and after your ritual focused on your goal, you will get to see your desires manifest.</u>

There are some examples of prayers, conjurations, oils, and perfumes you can use on the next pages.

Prayers and Conjurations

EXAMPLE OF CONJURATION

O ye Spirits, ye I conjure by the Power, Wisdom, and Virtue of the Spirit of God, by the uncreate Divine Knowledge, by the vast Mercy of God, by the Strength of God, by the Greatness of God, by the Unity of God; and by the Holy Name of God EHEIEH, which is the root, trunk, source, and origin of all the other Divine Names, whence they all draw their life and their virtue, which Adam having invoked, he acquired the knowledge of all created things.

I conjure ye by the Indivisible Name IOD, which marketh and expresseth the Simplicity and the Unity of the Nature Divine, which Abel having invoked, he deserved 2 to escape from the hands of Cain his brother.

I conjure ye by the Name TETRAGRAMMATON ELOHIM, which expresseth and signifieth the Grandeur of so lofty a Majesty, that Noah having pronounced it, saved himself, and protected himself with his whole household from the Waters of the Deluge.

I conjure ye by the Name of God EL Strong and Wonderful, which denoteth the Mercy and Goodness of His Majesty Divine, which Abraham having invoked, he was found worthy to come forth from the Ur of the Chaldeans.

I conjure ye by the most powerful Name of ELOHIM GIBOR, which showeth forth the Strength of God, of a God All Powerful, Who punisheth the crimes of the wicked, Who seeketh out and chastiseth the iniquities of the fathers upon the children unto the third and fourth generation; which Isaac having invoked, he was found worthy to escape from the Sword of Abraham his father.

I conjure ye and I exorcise ye by the most holy Name of ELOAH VA-DAATH, which Jacob invoked when in great trouble, and was found worthy to bear the Name of Israel, which signifieth Vanquisher of God and he was delivered from the fury of Esau his brother.

I conjure ye by the most potent Name of EL 3 ADONAI TZABAOTH, which is the God of Armies, ruling in the Heavens, which Joseph invoked, and was found worthy to escape from the hands of his Brethren.

I conjure ye by the most potent name of ELOHIM TZABAOTH, which expresses piety, mercy, splendour, and knowledge of God, which Moses invoked, and he was found worthy to deliver the People Israel from Egypt, and from the servitude of Pharaoh.

I conjure ye by the most potent Name of SHADDAI, which signifieth doing good unto all; which Moses invoked, and having struck the Sea, it divided into two parts in the midst, on the right hand and on the left. I conjure ye by the most holy Name of EL 1 CHAT, which is that of the Living God, through the virtue of which alliance with us, and redemption for us have been made; which Moses invoked and all the waters returned to their prior state and enveloped the Egyptians, so that not one of them escaped to carry the news into the Land of Mizraim.

Lastly, I conjure ye all, ye rebellious Spirits, by the most holy Name of God ADONAI MELEKH, which Joshua invoked, and stayed the course of the Sun in his presence, through the virtue of Methratton, 2 its principal Image; and by the troops of Angels who cease not to cry day and night, QADOSCH, QADOSCH, QADOSCH, ADONAI ELOHIM TZABAOTH (that is, Holy, Holy, Holy, Lord God of Hosts, Heaven and Earth are full of Thy Glory); and by the Ten Angels who preside over the Ten Sephiroth, by whom God communicateth and extendeth His influence over lower things, which are KETHER, CHOKMAH, BINAH, GEDULAH, GEBURAH, TIPHERETH, NETZACH, HOD, YESOD, and MALKUTH.

I conjure ye anew, O Spirits, by all the Names of God, and by all His marvellous work; by the heavens; by the earth; by the sea; by the depth of the Abyss, and by that firmament which the very Spirit of God hath moved; by the sun and by the stars; by the waters and by the seas, and all which they contain; by the winds, the whirlwinds, and the tempests; by the virtue of all herbs, plants, and stones; by all which is in the heavens, upon the earth, and in all the Abysses of the Shades.

I conjure ye anew, and I powerfully urge ye, O Demons, in whatsoever part of the world ye may be, so that ye shall be unable to remain in air, fire, water, earth, or in any part of the universe, or in any pleasant place which may attract ye; but that ye come promptly to accomplish our desire, and all things that we demand from your obedience.

I conjure ye anew by the two Tables of the Law, by the five books of Moses, by the Seven Burning Lamps on the Candlestick of Gold before the face of the Throne of the Majesty of God, and by the Holy of Holies wherein the KOHEN HA-GADUL was alone permitted to enter, that is to say, the High-Priest.

I conjure ye by Him Who hath made the heavens and the earth, and Who hath measured those heavens in the hollow of His hand, and enclosed the earth with three of His fingers, Who is seated upon the Kerubim and upon the Seraphim; and by the Kerubim, which is called the Kerub, which God constituted and placed to guard the Tree of Life, armed with a flaming sword, after that Man had been driven out of Paradise.

I conjure ye anew, Apostates from God, by Him Who alone hath performed great wonders; by the Heavenly Jerusalem; and by the Most Holy Name of God in Four Letters, and by Him Who enlighteneth all things and shineth upon all things by his Venerable and Ineffable Name, EHEIEH ASHER EHEIEH; that ye come immediately to execute our desire, whatever it may be.

I conjure ye, and I command ye absolutely, O Demons, in whatsoever part of the Universe ye may be, by the virtue of all these Holy Names:--

ADONAI, 1 YAH, HOA, EL, ELOHA, ELOHINU, ELOHIM, EHEIEH, MARON, KAPHU, ESCH, INNON, AVEN, AGLA, HAZOR, EMETH, YAII, ARARITHA, YOVA, HA-KABIR, MESSIACH, IONAH, MAL-KA, EREL, KUZU, MATZPATZ, EL SHADDAI; and by all the Holy Names of God which have been written with blood in the sign of an eternal alliance.

I conjure ye anew by these other Names of God, Most Holy and unknown, by the virtue of which Names ye tremble every day:--BARUC, 2 BACURABON, PATACEL, ALCHEEGHEL, AQUACHAI, HOMORION, EHEIEH, ABBATON, CHEVON, CEBON, OYZROYMAS, CHAI, EHEIEH, ALBAMACHI, ORTAGU, NALE, ABELECH (or HELECH), YEZE (or SECHEZZE); that ye come quickly and without any delay into our presence from every quarter and every climate of the world wherein ye may be, to execute all that we shall command ye in the Great Name of God.

EXAMPLE OF PRAYER

O LORD God, Holy Father, Almighty and Merciful One, Who hast created all things, Who knowest all things and can do all things, from Whom nothing is hidden, to Whom nothing is impossible; Thou Who knowest that we perform not these ceremonies to tempt Thy power, but that we may penetrate into the knowledge of hidden things; we pray Thee by Thy Sacred Mercy to cause and to permit that we may arrive at this understanding of secret things, of whatever nature they may be, by Thine aid, O Most Holy ADONAI, Whose Kingdom and Power shall have no end unto the Ages of the Ages. Amen.

The Prayer being finished, let the Exorcist lay his hand upon the Pentacles, while one of the Disciples shall hold open before him the Book wherein are written the prayers and conjurations proper for conquering, subduing, and reproving the Spirits. Then the Master, turning towards each Quarter of the Earth, and raising his eyes to Heaven, shall say:

O Lord, be Thou unto me a strong tower of refuge, from the sight and assaults of the Evil Spirits.

After which let him turn again towards the Four Quarters of the Earth and towards each let him utter the following words:

Behold the Symbols and Names of the Creator, which give unto ye for ever Protection and Inspiration. Obey then, by the virtue of these Holy Names, and by these Mysteries of Mysteries.

After this he shall see the Spirits come from every side. But in case they are occupied in some other place, or that they cannot come, or that they are unwilling to come: then let him commence afresh to invoke them after the following manner and let the Exorcist be assured that even were they bound with chains of iron and with fire, they could not refrain from coming to accomplish his will.

ANOTHER PRAYER

I HAVE invoked thee, O Sun, in the midst of the high heavens.

Thou art in the shadow of the cedar and thy feet rest on the summits.

The countries have called thee eagerly, they have directed their looks towards thee.

O Friend, thy brilliant light illuminates every land, overthrowing all that impedes thee, assemble the countries, for thou, O Sun, knowest their boundaries.

Thou who annihilatest falsehood, who dissipated the evil influence of wonders, omens, sorceries, dreams, evil apparitions, who turnest to a happy issue malicious designs, who annihilatest men and countries that devote themselves to fatal sorceries, I have taken refuge in thy presence.

Do not allow those who make spells, and are hardened, to arise.

Frighten their heart,

Settle also, O Sun, light of the great gods

Right into my marrow, O Lords of breath, that I may rejoice, even I.

May the gods who created me take my hands!

Direct the breath of my mouth!

My hands direct them also, Lord, light of the legions of the heavens. Sun, O Judge!

AND ANOTHER PRAYER

God's life is my life and I vibrate with harmony and

wholeness. I am free with the knowledge that all is good; I

am therefore perfectly whole and well.

I acknowledge Thy presence and power, O blessed Spirit; in

Thy divine wisdom now erase my mortal limitations and from

Thy pure substance of love bring into manifestation my

world, according to Thy perfect law.

Hear me now. I implore you to infuse this seal with your power so it can help me with (state purpose).

I humbly thank you for your infinite presence and love.

AND ANOTHER PRAYER

I am brave and bold with the knowledge that I am Spirit and

therefore not subject to any opposing power.

Plenty and prosperity are mine by inheritance from God and

by my steady persistent word I now bring them into

manifestation.

Oh Holy Spirit make this seal powerful for my use. I thank you for all your light, love, and protection. Amen.

Examples of Oils

FOR MONEY AND BUSINESS:	FOR LOVE:
Fast Money	Come to Me
Improve Business	Hummingbird
Opportunity is Knocking	Patchouli
Pay Me Now	Sticky-Sticky
Steady Job	Tied-On-To-Me

FOR GOOD LUCK:	SPECIAL PETITIONS:
Attract-Attract	Blessed
Double Good Luck	Holy Death
I'll Succeed	Saint Benedict
Road Opener	Saint Jude
Unblocking	

FOR DOMINATION:	FOR PROTECTION:
Be Quiet	Destroy Everything
Holy Death	Law on my Side
Martha Dominadora	Protection
Restless	Protection From Envy
Reversible	Rue
	Win In Court

Examples of Perfumes

FOR MONEY AND BUSINESS:	FOR LOVE:
Fast Money	Bridal Veil
Improve Business	Charm and Enchantment
Steady Job	Come to Me
	Hummingbird

FOR GOOD LUCK:	SPECIAL PETITIONS:
Macaw Bird	7 African Powers
Triple Good Luck	Holy Death
Unblocking	Saint Cyprian

FOR DOMINATION:	FOR PROTECTION:
Stuck-On-Me	Protection from Envy
Tied-On-To-Me	Win in Court
Weed of Love	

Examples of Candles

FOR MONEY & BUSINESS:	FOR LOVE:
Attract Customers	7 Drops of Love
Better Business	Adam & Eve
Don Juan Mr. Money	Come To Me
Fast Money	Honey of Love
Wealth & Prosperity	Love Drawing
	Patchouli

FOR GOOD LUCK:	SPECIAL PETITIONS:
Cleansing	7 Archangels
Double Good Luck	Child of Atocha
Garlic	Conqueror
Good Luck & Protection	Divine Trinity
Road Opener	Just Judge
Triple Good Luck	Most Powerful Hand
	Saint Jude

FOR DOMINATION:	FOR PROTECTION:
Black Destroyer	7x7 Against All
Control	Against Evil
Dume Destroyer	Balance of Justice
Holy Death	Coyote
I Can and You Can't	Hex Breaker
Restless	Protection From Envy
Reversible	Win in Court

Alchemical Symbols of the Seasons

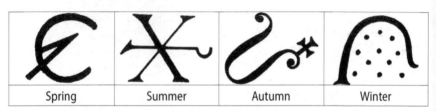

| Spring | Summer | Autumn | Winter |

Alchemical Symbols of the Elements

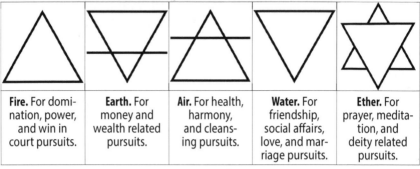

| **Fire.** For domination, power, and win in court pursuits. | **Earth.** For money and wealth related pursuits. | **Air.** For health, harmony, and cleansing pursuits. | **Water.** For friendship, social affairs, love, and marriage pursuits. | **Ether.** For prayer, meditation, and deity related pursuits. |

Astrological Seals of the Days
with their Planet, Zodiac Signs, and Angels

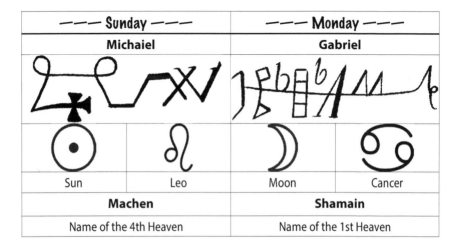

––– Sunday –––		––– Monday –––	
Michaiel		**Gabriel**	
Sun	Leo	Moon	Cancer
Machen		**Shamain**	
Name of the 4th Heaven		Name of the 1st Heaven	

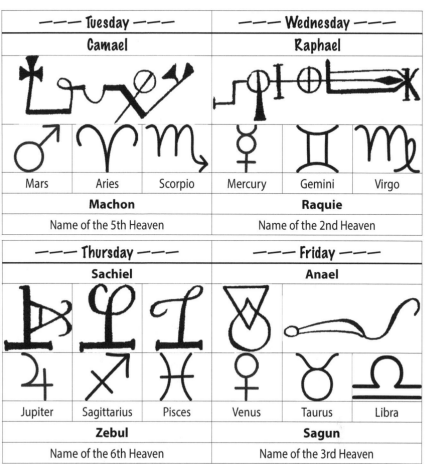

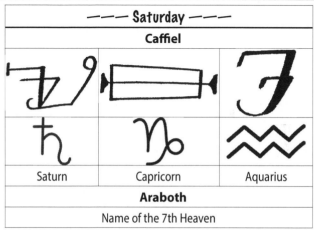

Seals of the Planets

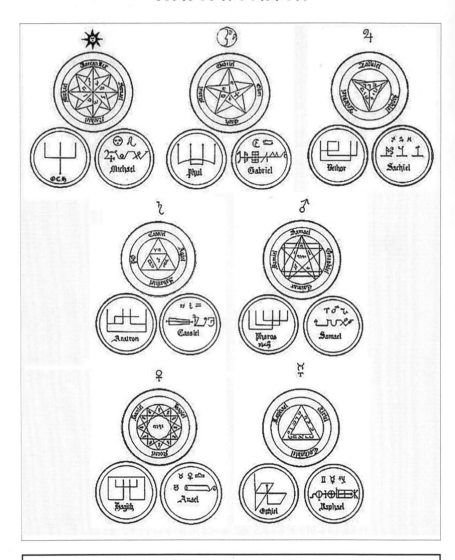

The Pentacles Of The Seven Planets, The Seals, and Characters Of The Planetary Angels. The seven large circles are the planets, while the two smaller circles under each contain the seal, and the character of the controlling intelligence of the planet.

Zodiac Constellations

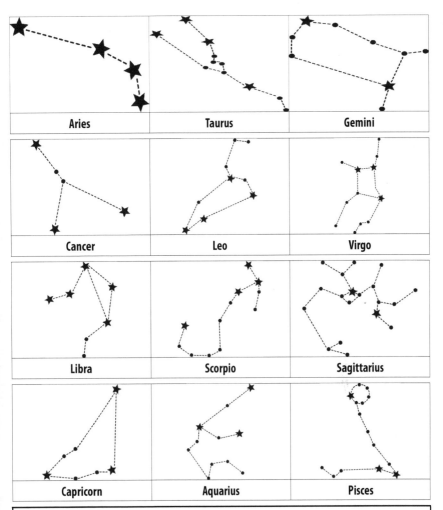

Zodiac Constellations. According to Wikipedia, the zodiac was in use back in the Roman era, based on concepts inherited by Hellenistic astronomy from Babylonian astronomy of the Chaldrean period (mid-1st century BC), which in turn derived from an earlier system of lists of stars, as observed by ancient astronomers. **These constellations were the basis for the study of each zodiacal sign.**

Astrological Signs and Symbols

These symbols can be used when preparing seals to attach them to your own sign or to the signs of those whom you're casting the spell for.

Hex Signs

Bright Day.	Redemption and Regeneration.	Good Luck and to Keep Away Evil.
Lucky Stars.	Faith and Goodwill.	Peace and Contentment.
Sun, Rain, and Fertility.	Success, Wealth, and Prosperity.	Wheel of Fortune.

Hex Signs are painted in colors and placed on the outside of houses or buildings. They first appeared in the USA in the early 19th century in the barns of farmers around the Pennsylvania area.

Colors have the following meanings:

Black. Protection. Rebirth.
Blue. Peace. Spirituality. Calm.
Brown. Earth. Strength. Birth. Creativity.
Green. Growth. Success. Ideas. Prosperity.
Orange. Abundance. Harvest. Security.
Purple. All Things Sacred. Religion. Transformation.
Red. Emotions: Love. Lust. Regeneration. Fertility.
White. Purity. Moon Power. Cleanliness. Free Flowing Energy.
Yellow. Health. Love. Sun. Playfulness. Connection To God.

Magic Tables of the Planets

4	14	15	1
9	7	6	12
5	11	10	8
16	2	3	13

Table of Jupiter. 4x4 Square. Numbers 1 to 16 Sum per row/column: 34. Grand total: 136. Used to attract good fortune in business, legal, personal, and religious affairs.

11	24	7	20	3
4	12	25	8	16
17	5	13	21	9
10	18	1	14	22
23	6	19	2	15

Table of Mars. 5x5 Square. Numbers 1 to 25 Sum per row/column: 65. Grand total: 325. Used to bring strength and courage needed to win battles or confrontations.

4	9	2
3	5	7
8	1	6

Table of Saturn. 3x3 Square. Numbers 1 to 9. Sum per row/column: 15. Grand total: 45. It is used by anyone who wants to achieve excellence on all of their endeavors.

22	47	16	41	10	35	4
5	23	48	17	42	11	29
30	6	24	49	18	36	12
13	31	7	25	43	19	37
38	14	32	1	26	44	20
21	39	8	33	2	27	45
46	15	40	9	34	3	28

Table of Venus. 7x7 Square. Numbers 1 to 49. Sum per row/column: 175. Grand total: 1,225. Used in all matters of love, friendship, and family affairs.

6	32	3	34	35	1
7	11	27	28	8	30
19	14	16	15	23	24
18	20	22	21	17	13
25	29	10	9	26	12
36	5	33	4	2	31

Table of the Sun. 6x6 Square. Numbers 1 to 36 Sum per row/column: 111. Grand total: 666. Used to conquer leadership. It brings in good health and great power.

8	58	59	5	4	62	63	1
49	15	14	52	53	11	10	56
41	23	22	44	48	19	18	45
32	34	38	29	25	35	39	28
40	26	27	37	36	30	31	33
17	47	46	20	21	43	42	24
9	55	51	12	13	54	50	16
64	2	3	61	60	6	7	57

Table of Mercury. 8x8 Square. Numbers 1 to 64. Sum per row/column: 260. Grand total: 2,080. Used for safe traveling and to sharpen communication skills.

37	78	29	70	21	62	13	54	5
6	38	79	30	71	22	63	14	46
47	7	39	80	31	72	23	55	15
16	48	8	40	81	32	64	24	56
57	17	49	9	41	73	33	65	25
26	58	18	50	1	42	74	34	66
67	27	59	10	51	2	43	75	35
36	68	19	60	11	52	3	44	76
77	28	69	20	61	12	53	4	45

Table of the Moon. 9x9 Square. Numbers 1 to 81 Sum per row/column: 369. Grand total: 3,321. Used in farming, new beginnings, and to settle disturbances.

These squares, from The Magus (1801), have one thing in common. If you sum up their rows, you will end up with the same total as the sum of each one of their columns.

Magic Squares of Abramelin 1/4

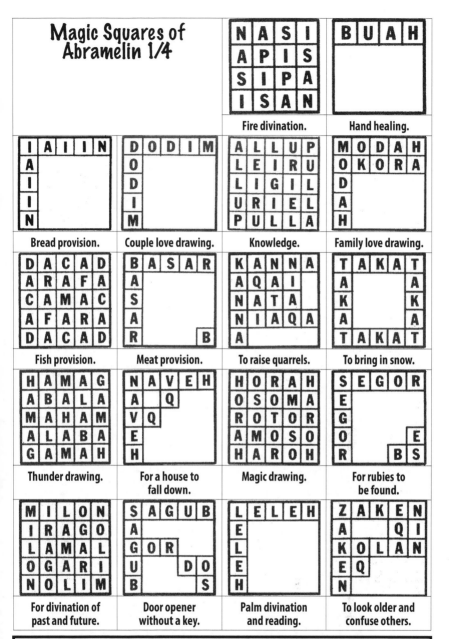

Magic Squares of Abramelin 2/4

L	E	C	H	E	M
E					
C	N	O	H	A	H
H					
E					
M	E	C	H	E	L

To have wine supply.

B	E	B	H	E	R
E	R	A	O	S	E
B	A	R	I	O	H
H	O	I	R	A	B
E	S	O	A	R	E
R	E	H	B	E	D

Relief from body pains.

S	A	G	R	I	R
A					
G					
R					
I					
R					

To bring in rain.

A	S	A	M	I	M
S					
A					
M	A	P	I	D	E
I					
M					

Uncover someone's riches.

H	A	P	P	I	R
A	M	A	O	S	I
P	A	R	A	O	P
P	O	A	R	A	P
I	S	O	A	M	A
R	I	P	P	A	H

Wound healing.

L	A	C	H	A	T
A					A
C					H
H					C
A					A
T	A	H	C	A	L

Heal from curses.

B	E	L	I	A	L
E	B	O	R	U	A
L	O	V	A	R	I
I	R	A	V	O	L
A	V	R	O	B	E
L	A	I	L	E	B

For jewels to be found.

C	A	L	L	A	H
A					
L	O	R	A	I	L
L					
A	G	O	U	P	A
H	A	L	L	A	C

To make others love you more.

T	E	L	A	A	H
E					A
L					L
A					A
A					A
H	A	A	L	E	T

To protect places from collapsing.

Q	E	B	H	I	R
E	R	A	I	S	A
B	A	Q	O	L	I
H	I	O	L	I	A
I	S	L	I	A	C
R	A	I	A	C	A

To gain other's respect and admiration.

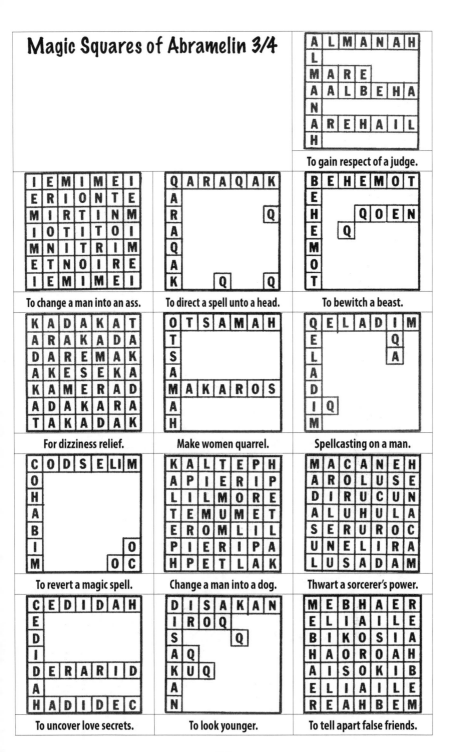

Magic Squares of Abramelin 4/4

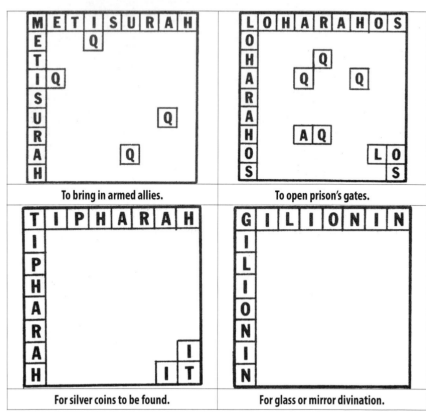

Feng Shui Five Elements

Seals of Solomon 1/4

The Seven Seals of Jupiter

			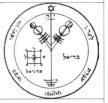
1. To attract wealth and prosperity in business.	2. To attract riches, honors, and peace of mind.	3. Protection from evil spirits that may linger around.	4. To gain and retain wealth and honors. Combine with #2.

5. Jacob's very own seal. Used to guarantee visions.	6. Protection from danger.	7. Protection from poverty.

The Seven Seals of Mars

			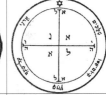
1. To guarantee enthusiasm, ambition, and great courage in physical matters.	2. Apply to affected areas to release a relentless healing power.	3. Use it to draw discord among others, and to outlast enemies.	4. To get vindication, even victory, in a confrontation of any kind.

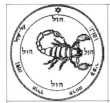		
5. To govern over demons.	6. Protection from harm, and to make enemies weapons turn on themselves.	7. Whisper El and Yial Divine Names' to bring confusion to known enemies.

Seals of Solomon 2/4

The Five Seals of Mercury

 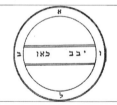 

1. To gain personal magnetism.

2. To overcome lost causes and insurmountable stakes.

3. Used by writers to sharpen literary skills.

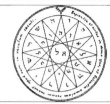 

4. To reach hidden thoughts and to gain knowledge of hidden things.

5. Unblocks roads, opens doors of any kind. Removes obstacles.

The Six Seals of the Moon

1. Opens even the strongest of doors or locks.

2. Protects from storms, hurricanes, earthquakes, or tornadoes.

3. Protection from danger of any type and deceitful attacks.

  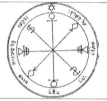

4. Protection from injuries intended to harm body or soul.

5. Protects from nightmares & restlessness. Induces revelatory dreams.

6. Place it under water to promote beautiful, restoring rain.

Seals of Solomon 3/4

The Seven Seals of Saturn

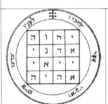  

1. To make other submissive to one's wishes.
2. To gain the upper hand with competitors or adversaries.
3. Protection from evil spirits and evil doers.
4. To bring in good news and to control others.

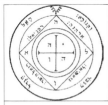  

5. Protection for home and possesions.
6. Make a foe be possessed by demons with these words: "Set thou a wicked one to be ruler over ____, and let Satan stand at his right hand."
7. To make others listen and fear the words of the bearer.

The Seven Seals of the Sun

1. This seal called "El Shaddai" makes the bearer's wishes come true.
2. To humble those who oppose the bearer's wishes or commands.
3. Draws glory, riches, and social standing to the bearer.
4. Makes foes or friends show their true colors and innermost thoughts.

5. Brings in Spirits to help the bearer travel to any place in short time.
6. Grants invisibility to the bearer at his request.
7. Helps the bearer be released from prisons real or of their own making.

Seals of Solomon 4/4

The Five Seals of Venus

1. Promotes good, long lasting friendships.	**2.** To receive all heart's wishes in matters of love.	**3.** To be bestowed with admiration, great respect, and love.

4. This seal will help the bearer to make any person come to him or her even against their will.	**5.** To be shown to a person in order to arouse in him/her great passion and strong desire.

Solomon Seals were passed down from generation to generation as hidden or lost books of Moses of the Hebrew Bible. They come from a grimoire containing drawings used in magical spells to secure good fortune and good health to the spellcaster and their loved ones. These seals contain Talmudic magic, names, words, and ideograms some written in Hebrew and some with letters from the Latin alphabet.

Seals of the Spirits 1/6

		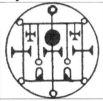	
Agares #2. To bring back someone who strayed. Also used on mighty people to bring down to their knees.	**Aim #23.** To cause destruction by fire. To find hard to come by answers. To learn Machiavellian maneuvers.	**Alloces #52.** This spirit can be sent to exert revenge on foes and enemies.	**Andras #63.** A mighty destroyer. He can cause financial and personal destruction to an enemy.

Andrealphus #65. Master of Mathematics. He can transform people into birds.	**Andromalius #72.** He finds lost things, reveals secrets, and uncovers plots against the carrier.	**Asmoday #32.** You ask questions, he answers. He helps you know innermost thoughts of others.	**Bathin #18.** He knows the virtues of plants and stones, and helps in astral travelling.
			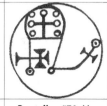
Bifrons #46. He brings spirits of the dead to answer questions, moves corpses, and imparts knowledge on herbs, stones, astrology, and mathematics.	**Camio or Caim #53.** Will teach you how to communicate with animals and help you unveil mysteries from other planes.	**Crocell #49.** Creates noise to cause chaos and confusion among foes. Teacher of art, geometry, history, and literature.	**Dantalion #71.** He brings out innermost thoughts of others. Creates chimeras to influence others' minds.

> **The Seals of the Spirits**, also called the 72 Seals of Solomon, have trascended in parallel within Jewish mysticism, Islamic mysticism, and Western occultism. These seals were used in casting spells to secure power, riches, and glory to the possessor. Some of them allegedly were used in black magic spells; others in white magic spells. Some of them have both energies. In any case, be mindful when casting black magic because that dark energy might hang around or come back to haunt the spellcaster.

Seals of the Spirits 2/6

Decarabia #69. He rules over plants and stones. He governs over 30 legions of Spirits.	**Focalor #41.** He governs over wind and water. He sinks ships, and can cause eath by drowning.	**Furfur #34.** He governs over thunder and lightning and reveals other's secret thoughts.	**Glasya-Labolas #25.** He grants invisibility. Can induce murder and death. Master of science and occult wisdom.
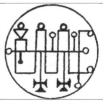			
Haagenti #48. Powerful alchemist who transforms water into wine and all metals into gold.	**Halphas or Malthus #38.** Governs over war. He can punish those who have wronged the sorcerer.	**Haures, Hauras, Havres, or Flauros #64.** He protects the sorcerer and can destroy one's foes.	**Leraie or Leraikha #14.** Prevents wounds from healing. He breaks up love in married or unmarried couples.

Malphas #39. He can create anything you ask him for, and he can advise you of your enemies' desires.	**Murmur or Murmus #54.** He can teach you philosophy. He can bring back the souls of the dead to answer questions.	**Ose or Voso #57.** He can change anyone into any shape without their knowledge.	**Paimon #9.** Grants the sorcerer the power to dominate and subjugate others.

Seals of the Spirits 3/6

	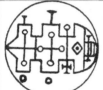		
Purson #20. Reads past and future and helps the sorcerer know what others are thinking.	**Raum or Räum #40.** Can bring destruction to or help you reconcile with enemies. Will steal money on behalf of the sorcerer.	**Ronové #27.** Master of languages will reel into submission a person posed against the sorcerer.	**Sabnock #43.** Protector of the military can make petty disputes escalate into full blown wars and prevent wounds from healing.
		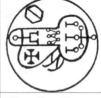	
Samigina or Gamigm #4. Teacher of liberal sciences can reveal souls of the dead who died in sin.	**Seere, Sear, or Seir #70.** Can bring about anything to happen instantly and modify time to suit the sorcerer's needs.	**Shan, Shax, Shaz or Shass #44.** Can take away sight, hearing, or understanding from anyone. Can steal money, find stolen goods, and bring someone close to assist the sorcerer.	**Sitri #12.** Can cause man or woman to show themselves naked. He inflames passions, love, and lust.
			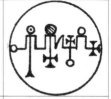
Valefor #6. Occult healer can cure all illnesses with magic. Can change others into animals. Grants the sorcerer skilled hands and sharpness of mind.	**Vepar or Vephar #42.** Master of the waters. He can bring about disaster and death attached to storms at sea.	**Viné or Vinea #45.** Will reveal the identity of other witches and sorcerers to the possessor. Can protect the sorcerer and destroy their enemies.	**Zagan #61.** He can make men witty. Can turn wine into water, blood into wine, or metals into coins.

Seals of the Spirits 4/6

Amdusias or Amdukias #67. Will send someone close to assist in a secret endeavor. Can prevent a tree from producing fruit.	**Amon #7.** Promoter of love and good will. Can help the sorcerer to reconcile with enemies. Foretells the future.	**Amy, or Avnas #58.** Helps uncover hidden treasures. Promotes wealth and good fortune. Enlightens in astrology issues.	**Astaroth #29.** Reveals the future through visions and dreams. Helps the sorcerer to uncover the unknown.
	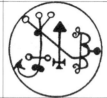		
Bael #1. Enlightens the mind of the bearer when he has to make a decision in a seemingly hopeless situation.	**Balam #51.** Grants the ability to use words in a clever and funny way with a sharper mind.	**Barbatos #8.** He can be invoked only under the sign of Saggittarius to heal emotional wounds and to strengthen relationships.	**Beleth, Bileth, or Bilet #13.** Facilitates marriage proposals and makes love flourish, and freely flow.

Belial #68. This spirit will help the sorcerer in all job related endeavors. Also, to achieve higher positions, receive praise, and get help from friends, even foes.	**Berith, Beale, Beal, Bofry, or Bolfry #28.** Reveals the future. Converts metals into gold. Helps the sorcerer to receive honors, recognition, and good social standing.	**Botis #17.** Grants protection from harm, envy, and hatred. Helps in decision making. Brings back harmony in the house. Strengthens courage.	**Buer #10.** Teaches logic and philosophy. Imparts cure for all maladies and diseases and helps recover from addictions, specially from alcohol.

Seals of the Spirits 5/6

Bune or Bimé #26. Grants the ability to use words with elegance and acuity. Brings in wealth and prosperity.	**Cimejes, Cimeies, or Kimaris #66.** Brings out hero traits to the bearer. Helps recover lost things. Teaches literature.	**Eligos #15.** Draws success in business and financial matters. Grants favors in legal issues and court cases.	**Foras #31.** Teaches knowledge on stones, and plants, as wll as logic. Helps recover lost things and promotes wealth and wisdom.
	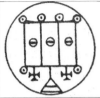	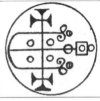	
Forneus #30. Grants protection from evildoers. Can draw love from enemies. Teaches sciences, arts, and languages.	**Furcas #50.** Teacher of philosophy and sciences. Helps the sorcerer to still his mind and get rid of fear.	**Gaap #33.** Helps in astral travels and to forsee the future. Makes polarizing emotions (love or hate) flow into an environment.	**Gremory or Gamori #56.** This spirit is the only one who appears as a woman, a beautiful one, and procures love of women, both young and old.
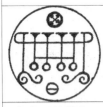	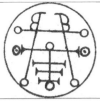		
Gusion #11. Helps the bearer receive honors and admiration from others, even from those who didn't care for him/her before.	**Ipos #22.** Can read past and present. Helps the bearer gain control, courage, and make long lasting friendships.	**Marax #21.** Brings in help from someone close. Procures knowledge in the magical use of stones, herbs, and astrology.	**Marbas #5.** Grants wisdom and helps the bearer find stolen or hidden things. Can either cause or cure diseases or maladies.

Seals of the Spirits 6/6

Marchosias #35. Helps the bearer get on top of arguments or quarrels. He takes the shape of a wolf.	**Naberius #24.** Helps recover lost honors or possesions. He will help you master the art of rhetoric or teach you Arts and Sciences.	**Oriax, or Orias #59.** Makes foes or enemies switch positions in favor of the bearer and gain a higher, more respected position.	**Orobas #55.** Helps to dominate others. Protects from slander and persecution. Casts away evil spirits or vindictive entities.
	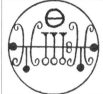		
Phenex or Pheynix #37. He is a poet that will obey all your requests. He is sweet, and speaks with the voice of a child.	**Sallos or Saleos #19.** He arouses desire and passion between the couple. He strengthens loyalty and fidelity.	**Stolas or Stolos #36.** He is the master of all knowledge in regards to plants, stones, and the stars. He takes the shape of a Raven.	**Volac, Volax, Valax, Valu, or Ualac #62.** You can ask him for help when you need to find a lost treasure, a good job, a good friend, or a lucky number.

Vapula, or Naphula #60. He can help you pass any exam in any subject or help you have an engaging conversation.	**Vassago #3.** He helps find lost or misplaced things, and gives you information of past, and future happenings.	**Vual, Uvall, or Voval #47.** He can adjust time at will. Will create friendship, love, and self esteem.	**Zepar #16.** He will bring together in love any couple. He dresses in red and can change the shape of others at will.

Egyptian Symbols 1/2

Heart.	To protect the heart from negative emotions.
Scarab.	Represents the relentless force of life.
Buckle.	For strength and power.
Tet.	All points protection and affirmation of power.
Pillow.	Protection from enemies.
Vulture.	Protection in the afterlife.
Life.	To rise above obstacles, even dead.
Collar of God.	To free oneself from limitations.
Scepter.	To bring in vigor, and renewal of youth.
Ladder.	To communicate with God.
Two Fingers.	To receive prompt help when needed.
Eye of Horus.	To bring in all types of blessings.
Shen or Rising Sun.	To bless beginnings, including life, business, & relationships.
Nefer.	To bring in happiness and good luck.
Serpent's head.	Protection from being bitten by poisonous creatures.
Menat.	To bring in joy and good health.
Sam.	To enjoy human pleasures and long lasting unions.
Eye of Ra.	Represents the sun. Used to get illumination from the goddess or female energy.
Steps.	To reach heaven on earth.
Frog.	Represents resurrection. Used after a crisis to bring life back to a situation.

Egyptian Symbols 2/2

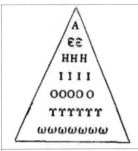

Amulets of the Archangels. These amulets were written on papyri to call upon the spirits, to ask them to draw light from darkness, dispose of everything negative, and hear the voice of the possessor; to loosen chains and blinds; to bring in revelatory dreams, and to create favorable conditions for the petition of the possessor.

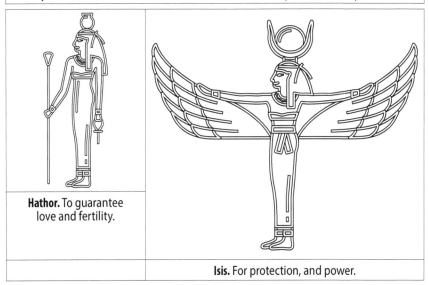

Hathor. To guarantee love and fertility.

Isis. For protection, and power.

Egyptian magic is mostly used to connect with the spiritual world, with loved ones who have parted or with spirits in general, as well as to secure help from them in different endeavors.

Seals of the Sage of the Pyramids 1/5

I. CONJURATION OF POWER. This seal serves for the conjuration of celestial and infernal powers. It should be embroidered in silver upon sky-blue satin. The evoking words are SIRAS, ETAR, BESANAR, at which multitudes of spirits will appear.	**II. WIN THE FEMALE.** Gives the love and complaisance of the entire female sex. It should be embroidered in silver on black satin. Evoking words are NADES, SURADIS, MANINER, pronounced with the seal held on the left hand-pressed against the lips.	**III. DISCOVER TREASURES.** Ensures their possession. The figure of the talisman should be embroidered in gold upon green satin. The evoking words are: ONAÏM, PERANTÈS, RASONASTOS.

IV. DISCOVER SECRETS. This seal helps you discover the most hidden secrets and enables its possessor to penetrate everywhere unseen. The talisman should be of violet satin, with the figures embroidered in silver. It must be held in the left hand, on which also the seal should be placed close to the ear, pronouncing the words NITAE, RADOU, SUNANDAM.	**V. POWER OF TRUTH.** Will make the most taciturn man unbosom himself to its possessor, whose enemies will also be forced to confess all their machinations. The talisman should be of gold-colored satin embroidered in gold. Place the seal on the left hand; talisman against right ear. Evoking words NOCTAR, RAIBAN & BRANTHER.	**VI. ACHIEVEMENT OF GOALS.** Sets to work enough genii for the immediate achievement of any work which the possessor may desire to undertake and for the stoppage of any which may oppose him. The talisman should be of lilac satin with the figures embroidered in shaded silk. The magical words are ZORAMI, ZAITUX, ELASTOT.

Seals of the Sage of the Pyramids 2/5

VII. PROTECTS FROM ACCIDENTS. Has the power to destroy everything; to cause the fall of hail, thunderbolts, and stars from heaven; to occasion earthquakes, storms, and so forth. At the same time it preserves the friends of the possessor from accidents. The figure of the talisman should be embroidered in silver upon poppy-red satin. The magical words are: (1) DITAU, HURANDOS, for works of destruction; (2) RIDAS, TALIMOL, to command the elements; (3) ATROSIS, NARPIDA, for the fall of hail, &c.; (4) UUSUR, ITAR, for earthquakes; (5) HISPEN, TROMADOR, for hurricanes and storms; (6) PARANTHES, HISTANOS, for the preservation of friends.

VIII. PROVIDES INVISIBILITY. Gives invisibility, so that God alone shall witness the actions of the possessor. Grants the power of passing through brick walls. The magical words are BENATIR, CARARKAU, DEDOS, ETINARMI. For each operation the ring must be placed upon a different finger of the right hand. The talisman is of yellow satin embroidered with black silk.

IX. PROTECTS THE TRAVELER. Transports the possessor to any part of the world and without danger. The potent words are RADITUS, POLASTRIEN, TERPANDU, OSTRATA, PERICATUR, ERMAS. The talisman is of dusty purple-colored satin embroidered with gold.

X. OPENS LOCKS. Opens all locks at a touch, despite whatever precautions have been taken to secure them. The magical words are SARITAP, PERNISOX, OTTARIM. The talisman is of deep blue satin embroidered with silver.

Seals of the Sage of the Pyramids 3/5

XI. READS OTHER'S THOUGHTS. Sets the possessor in any desired house and reads the thoughts of all persons, so that they can be helped or harmed at pleasure. The talisman is of light grey satin embroidered with gold. To know thoughts, place it on your head, breathe upon the seal, and say: O TAROT, NIZAEL, ESTARNAS, TANTAREZ. To serve those who are worthy: NISTA, SAPER, VISNOS, and they will forthwith enjoy every kind of prosperity. To punish your enemies or evil persons: XATROS, NIFER, ROXAS, TORTOS, and they will be immediately delivered to frightful torments.

XII. DESTROYS EVIL. Destroys all projects formed against the possessor and compels rebellious spirits. The talisman is of rose-colored satin embroidered with silver. It should be placed upon a table, the left hand imposed upon it; the seal should be on the right hand, and the operator, with bent head, should repeat in a low voice the words: SENAPOS, TERFITA, ESTAMOS, PERFITER, NOTARIN.

XIII. ENDOWS VIRTUE AND TALENT. Endows possessor with every virtue, talent, and the desire to do good. All substances of evil quality can be rendered excellent by means of it. For the first advantage, it is sufficient to raise up the talisman, having the seal upon the right hand, and to pronounce the words: TURAN, ESTONOS, FUZA. For the second, say: VAZOTAS, TESTANAR. The talisman should be of saffron colored satin embroidered with silver.

XIV. GIVES HEALING POWERS. Gives the knowledge of all minerals and vegetables, with their virtues and properties; gives the universal medicine and the faculty of healing all sick persons. The talisman is of orange-colored satin embroidered with silver. It should be worn upon the breast, and the seal in a locket (kerchief) around the neck, secured by means of a ribbon of flame-colored silk. The operative words are: RETERREM, SALIBAT, CRATARES, HISATER.

Seals of the Sage of the Pyramids 4/5

XV. PROTECTS FROM ANIMALS. Gives immunity from the most ferocious animals; gives the means of overcoming them; gives the knowledge of their language and drives mad animals away. The talisman should be of deep green satin embroidered with gold. For the first three objects, say: HOCATOS, IMORAD, SURATER, MARKILA. For the last: TRUMANTREM, RICONA, ESTUPIT, OXA.

XVI. COMMUNICATES WITH ALL. Gives discernment for the good or bad intentions of any person. The talisman is of black satin embroidered with gold. It should be placed upon the heart and the seal on the right hand. The words are: CROSTES, FURINOT, KATIPA, GARINOS.

XVII. GIVES KNOWLEDGE. Gives all talents and a profound knowledge of every art, so that the possessor will outshine the toil-worn experts though unqualified by scholarship. The talisman, which must be carried on the person, should be of white satin embroidered with black silk. The operative words are: RITAS, ONALUN, TERSORIT, OMBAS, SERPITAS, QUITATHAR, ZAMARATH, specifying the art which it is desired to possess.

XVIII. GIVES GOOD FORTUNE. In general and in Lotteries. The talisman is of cerise-colored satin embroidered with gold and silver. It should be bound upon the left arm by means of a white ribbon and the seal must be on the right hand. The words are: ROKES for a winning number, PILATUS for a double-ace, ZOTOAS for a denary, TULITAS for a quaternary, XATANITOS for a quinary. For cards the same potent formula should be repeated when shuffling for self or partner. Before beginning, touch your left arm with your right hand in the neighborhood of the talisman, and kiss the seal. These little contrivances can be effected, says the honest Grimoire, without exciting the notice of your opponent.

Seals of the Sage of the Pyramids 5/5

XIX. REPELS EVIL SPIRITS. Gives the power of directing all the infernal hosts against the enemies of its possessor. The talisman is of greyish-white satin, shaded. It may be worn in any manner and the words are: OSTHARIMAN, VISANTIPAROS, NOCTATUR.

XX. CONTROLS EVIL. Gives the knowledge of the counsels of Infernus and the means of rendering its projects abortive, but whether for the ultimate health and wealth of the operator's soul, there is no guarantee offered. The talisman is of red satin, with the center embroidered in gold, the border in silver, and the figures in black, and white silk. It should be worn upon the breast and the seal on the left hand. The words are: ACTATOS, CATIPTA, BEJOURAN, ITAPAN, MARNUTUS.

MAGIC ROD. This seal is used for protection. Should be worn on the clothes of the possessor to receive magical assistance, to be protected from hexes, and to maintain a good health, and a sunny disposition.

GOETIC CIRCLE. This circle should be worn on the clothes of the possessor while casting spells, to make all his desires come to pass, and his or her magic to be more effective.

SEALS OF THE SAGE OF THE PYRAMIDS pertain to the Book of Ceremonial Magic, which consists of three souces: The Art of Necromancy, The Science of Magical Talismans, and the Science of Bewitchment. These seals are used mostly as metal medals to secure power and command of all beings to the possessor. They can also be embroidered on fabric, leather, or any other material. They can be drawn on parchment, a scrap of thin wood, or metal. They are commonly used when casting spells and in any type of ceremonial magic.

Seals of the 6th & 7th Books of Moses 1/5

Schemhamphoras Holy Seal. Used to contact departed souls. For wealth and for vengeance endeavors.

Seal of Antiquelis. For wealth, honors, and good health endeavors.

Seal of Barbuelis. To master arts and occult knowledge.

Schemhamphoras Seal #1. Used to draw success in business and money matters.

Seal of Marbuelis. Used to mesmerize someone to obtain their secret knowledge.

Seal of Arielis. Used to make others do your bidding and to locate lost treasures.

Seal of Aziabelis. Used to attract friendship and power over others.

Schemhamphoras Seal #2. Used to draw mystical powers and divine guidance.

Seal of Mephistophilas. Used to overcome, dominate, and protect from enemies.

Seal of Rab Caleb. Used for medical assistance in obtaining health in body, mind, and spirit.

Seal of Orion. To make wishes come true. To attract success, honor, and respect from others.

Seal of Azielis. To draw out earthly treasures.

Seals of the 6th & 7th Books of Moses 2/5

Seal of Merbeulis or Seal of Special Attraction. To dominate and mesmerize others.

Seal of the Golden Candlestick. Protection from danger and firearms, making the bearer strong as steel.

Grand Symbol of Solomon. To gain wisdom, protection, and divine guidance in all matters.

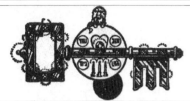

Master Key Seal. To draw good fortune, good health, and great success in all endeavors.

Seal of the Earth or Seal of Spiritual Assistance. To draw support from deities in all endeavors.

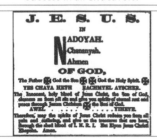

Seal of Jesus of God. For achieving victory in all endeavors under divine protection.

Seal of the Witness. To receive the most divine of all blessings from the All Mighty.

Seal of Power. Used to strengthen one's faith, influence others, and to restore one's good health.

Seal of the Sun or Seal of Honor and Wealth. Used by those who want to attract all the good things in life.

Seals of the 6th & 7th Books of Moses 3/5

Breastplate of Aaron. Used for protection from a violent death.

Breastplate of Moses. Protection from harm to the possessor and to his or her space.

Seal of the Air or Seal of Relief from Want. Used to have all basic needs covered. Used also by job seekers.

Seal of Good Luck. Anoint this seal and conceal it in your sleeve before playing games of chance to draw great success.

Seal of Fortune. To draw blessings and success in business, family, and personal affairs.

Seal of Great Generation. To draw honor, wealth, and to obtain promotions.

Seal of Fire. Used to draw popularity, influence, dominance, and to achieve power in any specific field.

Seal of Jupiter or Seal of Mystical Assistance. To settle disputes and to win in legal and court cases.

Seals of the 6th & 7th Books of Moses 4/5

Seal of Mars. Used to diffuse negative influences and to keep peace in love or friendship alliances.

Seal of Knowledge. Place this talisman under your pillow to have your questions answered during dreams or in daylight visions.

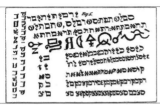

Seal of Long Life. This seal is used by those seeking to have a full, long, and happy life.

Seal of Mercury. Used for communication accuracy, to assure wealth, to unearth treasures, and to master alchemy and chemistry.

Seal of Saturn or Seal of Spiritual Good Luck. Used by gamblers who wish to attract favorable vibrations when drawing lucky numbers.

Seal of Treasure. Used to locate a lost object. Used also to bring in front of the possessor treasures hidden nearby.

Seal of Love. Used to surround the possessor with love. Used to enjoy a full and loving relationship with people surrounding the possessor.

Seal of Water or Seal of Great Fortune. Used to unearth precious metals from the earth, sunken ships from the water, or hidden treasures in abandoned places.

Seals of the 6th & 7th Books of Moses 5/5

Seal of the Spirits. Used to bring in help from the Spirits in cases when fast solutions are needed.

Seal of Treasures. Used to locate lost or stolen objects.

Seal of Venus or Seal of Secrets. Place this talisman under your pillow to have secrets revealed to you during your dreams and to protect your secrets from being revealed to others.

Seal of Treasure, Elevation, and Spiritual Redemption. Used to bring in peace to a person or place. Use it in your clothes or put it in the entrance of your home or business.

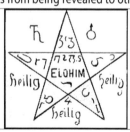

Great Pentagram Seal. To promote wisdom, a clear mind, and a bright disposition. Protection from black magic & deliverance from fear.

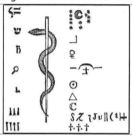

Seal of Magic. Assistance in magical endeavors to make one's wishes or requests come to reality.

The Crowned Serpent. Used to draw mighty power, dominance, and strength.

Seals of the 8th, 9th & 10th Books of Moses 1/4

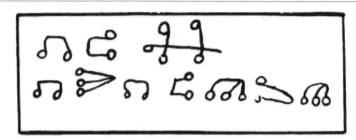

Seal to Gain the Love of All Living. "Write these names and seals on the palms of thy hands, and touch whomsoever thou wilt, and for the LOVE OF ALL LIVING, and to have power over all spirits call on this name: RUHIEL; or write it on parchment, and keep it on thy flesh, and this is what thou shalt say: 'AZOR AZARIAH LAHABIEL HAZAM Y Y Y YEHO'."

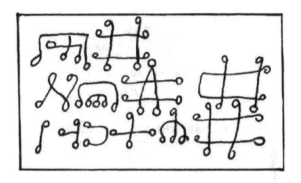

Seal so that the devil shall smite an enemy. "Take a stone and throw it to a dog which shall bite it; on it draw these symbols; throw it in the house of thine enemy and thou shalt see wonders."

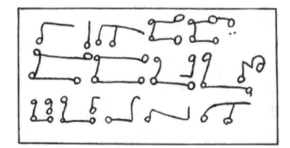

Seal to wreak vengeance upon an enemy. "Take this seal and wash it with water until it is clean, and taking the water thereof, and sprinkle it in the house of the enemy on the second night of the week or the fourth of the week at the seventh hour."

Seals of the 8th, 9th & 10th Books of Moses 2/4

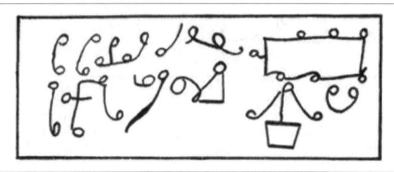

Seal for Love. "Write on parchment and burn it in a great fire: "Ye shall put love for N_____, son of _____, into the heart of N_____, daughter of N_____.""

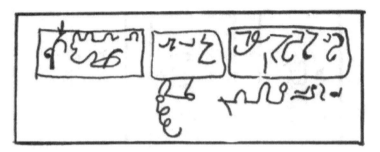

Seal For Whoever Wisheth For A Woman And Her Father Will Not Give Her. "Write on the back of the Seal the name of the daughter, and that man who will not give her to him and thou shall burn it in a fire."

3 Seals For Love Between A Man and His Wife. "Write these seals on three leaves in the name of N_____, son of _____, into the heart of N_____, daughter of N_____, and he shall burn one each day."

Seals of the 8th, 9th & 10th Books of Moses 3/4

Talisman for Protection. This talisman shows 7 figures which represent the Archangels Gabriel, Michael, Raphael, Uriel, Jhudiel, Barachel, and Sealtiel.

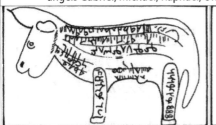 

Amulets of the Druses. These amulets symbolize the sign of Taurus. They were used to protect all property and to assure the possessor of wealth, prosperity, and all things related to earthly possesions, such as inheritances, treasures, and so forth.

Seal of Power. This seal has words of power written on it that "hath effect upon the heart of the Gods", enabling the possessor to compel the spirits to do his bidding.

Seal to recover hidden or buried treasures. This Talisman was exerted for the Ancient Syrians to enable the possessors to recover from the ruins of cities, buildings, and the bottom of wells, subterranean treasures, even those guarded by certain Genii.

Seals of the 8th, 9th & 10th Books of Moses 4/4

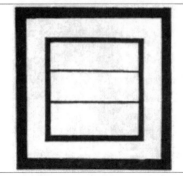

Protection Amulet. This Magical Design was known as the Protective Square, according to Lindsay. It consisted of a square, within a square, the former being divided into 3 compartments after the plan of a double walled, and many chambered castle indicating the protective character of the charm.

The Magic Bough. A charm against evil.

Holy Death Elements

Owl. Wisdom.	**Scale.** Justice.	**Earth Orb.** Success. Power.
Lamp. Clarity.	**Scythe.** Hex breaking. Protection.	**Hourglass.** Awarenes. Caution. Being wise with your time.

Sacred Geometry

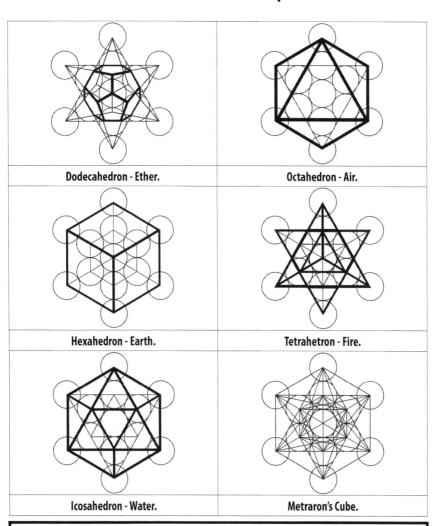

Dodecahedron - Ether.	Octahedron - Air.
Hexahedron - Earth.	Tetrahetron - Fire.
Icosahedron - Water.	Metraron's Cube.

Sacred Geometry is based on the observation of nature and on the belief that God created the world with perfect, well calibrated patterns. Physics and cosmology have studied these patterns in trying to make sense of the universe.

Sacred Geometry is used in the construction of religious structures such as churches, temples, mosques, pagodas, holy wells, and sacred groves. You can use it to create your altar or your sacred space for ceremonial magic or simply for yoga and meditation.

Shields of the Saints 1/8

Sacred Heart of Jesus. Used to restore and to preserve good health.	**Saint Anthony.** To guarantee good luck.	**Saint Basil.** Day and night protection during travels.

Saint Cyril. For wealth and prosperity.	**Saint Expedite.** For quick answers and to quickly find a job.	**Saint Mary.** To be rid of sickness and maladies.

Saint Marie Magdalene. To attract and hold on to love.	**Saint Michael.** To conquer all obstacles.	**Saint Peter.** To achieve success in a speedy way.

How to use the Shields:
Make a copy of the shield you want to use.
Write on the back your petition in positive words:
"Improve health", "Steady Job", "Wealth & Prosperity", etc.
Sprinkle a little ordinary table salt on the paper saying: "I purify you" as you do so.
Hold the shield up between your hands as if in a manner of prayer, and close your eyes:

"Great Universal Power, let this Shield of_____ grant me
what I need and want in a perfect way. Amen".

Now carry with you the shield without folding it. When your wish has come true, burn the Shield, and cast the ashes to the wind. Be grateful, and be blessed.
-*-
In the Catholic Church, most saints have some symbol associated with their ministry. These shields come from the earliest Church clergy.

-----> In the next pages you will find symbols of the Apostles, the Saints and <-----
Titles of Mary, Mother of Jesus, which you can mix and match to make your own shields.

DIY Shields of the Saints 2/8

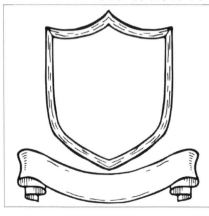

You can use the drawing on the left to prepare your own shields with the symbols of the Apostles, Virgin Mary's many representations, or Saints, according to your preferences.

Draw the image of the symbol on the center, write the name of the selected deity, and use the shield per the instructions on the introduction of this section.

These shields can be used for rituales, spells, amulets, or for prayer.

Symbols of the Apostles

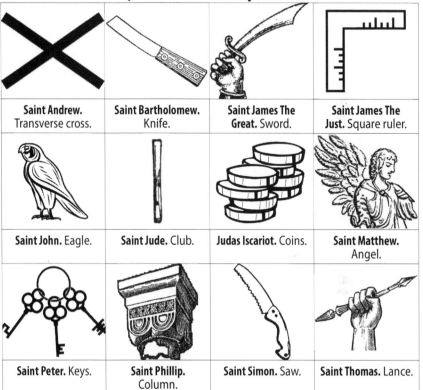

Saint Andrew. Transverse cross.	**Saint Bartholomew.** Knife.	**Saint James The Great.** Sword.	**Saint James The Just.** Square ruler.
Saint John. Eagle.	**Saint Jude.** Club.	**Judas Iscariot.** Coins.	**Saint Matthew.** Angel.
Saint Peter. Keys.	**Saint Phillip.** Column.	**Saint Simon.** Saw.	**Saint Thomas.** Lance.

Symbols of the Titles of Mary Mother of Jesus 3/8

Symbols of the Titles of Mary Mother of Jesus 4/8

Symbols of the Saints 5/8

Symbols of the Saints 6/8

Symbols of the Saints 7/8

Symbols of the Saints 8/8

Saint Monica. Tears.	Saint Nicholas. Cross.	Saint Pantaleon. Nailed hands.	Saint Patrick. Shamrock.
Saint Paul. Scroll.	Saint Rita of Cascia. Thorn.	Saint Roch. Dog.	Saint Rose of Lima. Anchor.
Saint Sebastian. Arrows.	Saint Teresa of Avila. Heart.	Saint Therese of Lisieux. Cross and rose.	Saint Thomas Aquinas. Ox.
Saint Vincent de Paul. Children.	Saint Vincent Ferrer. Pulpit.	Saint Vitus. Palm.	

Gnostic Seals 1/2

The Gorgon. Used to protect women and children especially during pregnancy.

The Abraxas-god. With the inscription "Son of the Universe". Also called "Eternal Son". Used for protection from all evil spirits.

The Agathodemon Serpent. Surrounded by triplets of the sacred animals of Egypt, all paying adoration to God. Used to increase the faith of the possessor.

Seal of Saint Servatius. Protection from foot trouble, and for healing all leg and foot ailments.

The Abraxas-god mounted in the chariot of the Sun. This talisman is used when power and command are needed to control a situation.

The "Great Names" Iao and Abraxas. Placed within a coiled serpent, emblem of Eternity. Used to make relationships and businesses live long, happy lives.

Horus, the Vernal Sun. He is seated on the lotus, receiving the adoration of the Baboon. Used for protection in quarrels, wars, disputes, and disagreements.

The Sun in his car. With the orb in his hand, he is saluted in the legend as "Thou art our Father!" To guarantee that all basic needs are covered every day.

Luna. The Moon. Used to have revelatory dreams, and to have questions answered while being asleep.

Gnostic Seals 2/2

Isis. One lotus on her brow, holding a sceptre. Used for magical protection.

Caduceus, within a myrtle wreath. Protection from demons.

Evil Eye. Talisman used from protection against envy and the evil eye.

Apollo. Used to attain and preserve good health.

Bishop Seffrid's Talismanic Ring. Depicting Abraxas-god found in his tomb. Preserved in the Cathedral Library, Chichester.

The Agathodemon. With the legend "I am Chnumis, Sun of the Universe, 700." Personal talisman. Possessor will add his personal number garnered from his name.

Serapis and Agathodemon. For good luck, good health, and wisdom.

The Sphinx. Used during initiation ceremonies and rituals.

<--- **Harpocrates.** To silence gossip, slander, and evil doers.

Dove with Olive Branch. For truce, reconciliation, and peace among parties.--->

7 Chakras Symbols

Sahasrara or Crown Chakra. Highest spiritual center, pure consciousness. When the feminine Kundalini Shakti rises to this point, it unites with the masculine Shiva, giving self-realization and samadhi. In esoteric Buddhism, it is called Mahasukha, the petal lotus of "Great Bliss" corresponding to the fourth state of Four Noble Truths.

Ajna or Third Eye Chakra. Guru chakra, or in New Age usage third-eye chakra, the subtle center of energy, where the tantra guru touches the seeker during the initiation ritual. He or she commands the awakened kundalini to pass through this center.

Vishuddha or Throat Chakra. 16 petals covered with the sixteen Sanskrit vowels. Associated with the element of space (akasha). The residing deity is Panchavaktra shiva, with 5 heads, 4 arms, and the Shakti is Shakini. In esoteric Buddhism, it is called Sambhoga, and is generally considered to be the petal lotus of "Enjoyment" corresponding to the third state of Four Noble Truths.

Anahata or Heart Chakra. Within it is a yantra of two intersecting triangles, a hexagram, or a union of the male and female. Element of air (vayu). Presiding deity: Ishana Rudra Shiva; the Shakti is Kakini. In esoteric Buddhism, it is called Dharma, and is considered to be the petal lotus of "Essential nature", corresponding to the second state of Four Noble Truths.

Manipura or Navel Chakra. For the Nath yogi meditation system, this is described as the Madhyama-Shakti or the intermediate stage of self-discovery. This chakra is represented as a downward pointing triangle representing fire in the middle of a lotus with ten petals. The presiding deity is Braddha Rudra, with Lakini as the Shakti.

Svadhishthana or Sexual Organs Chakra. Represented with a lotus within which is a crescent moon symbolizing the water element. The presiding deity is Brahma, with the Shakti being Rakini (or Chakini). In esoteric Buddhism, it is called Nirmana, the petal lotus of "Creation", corresponding to the first state of Four Noble Truths.

Muladhara or Root Chrakra. Dormant Kundalini is said to be resting here, wrapped 3 and a half, or 7 to 12 times, around the black Svayambhu linga, the lowest of three obstructions to her full rising (also known as knots or granthis). A four-petaled lotus with a yellow square at its center. Element: earth. The seed syllable is Lam for the earth element. All sounds, words, and mantras in their dormant form rest in the muladhara chakra, where Ganesha resides, while the Shakti is Dakini.

The chakra system originated in India between 1500 and 500 BC in the oldest text called the Vedas. Part of this description is from (*) https://en.wikipedia.org/wiki/Chakra

Power Squares

1	9	2	5	4
9	6	5	3	3

Telecommunication. During 7 days, repeat these numbers all day long to yourself. On the night of the 8th day, before falling sleep, repeat the numbers, and ask to be awaken at the time this person is receptive to your words. You will then wake up during the wee hours. When you wake up, with your eyes closed, talk to this person, and he/she will listen to you no matter how far they are from you.

R	A	I	Z	I
I	Z	I	A	R
A	Z	B	G	D
B	M	M	J	M

Avenger. When you're alone, and uninterrupted, light a candle. Four hours later, write these squares on a parchment paper. Hold it with your hands, and repeat: "Raizi", once to the north, once to the west, once to the east, and once to the south. Burn the square in the flame of a candle. Your foe will get their due for all harm inflicted upon your person or property.

1	21	63	7
21	7	1	21
9	19	91	9
12	4	6	8

Stay where you are. To prevent a person from straying away, write this square on a green cloth with golden or yellow ink. Hold the square on the left hand, and when you have that person in front of you, repeat these numbers 9 times, either aloud or just to yourself.

1	5	8	A	O
7	9	1	O	A
1	8	5	O	O
8	5	1	O	A

Alchemist. This square was used by magicians who were casting spells to change base metals into precious metals like silver and gold. It is also used to strengthen your magical powers while casting any type of spell.

S	D	D	D	C
H	T	L	T	B
S	D	D	D	C
H	T	L	T	B

Protection from evil. Write this table in a cloth, and sew it to the left sleeve so you're protected from evil spirits or entities while spell casting or performing magical rituals.

6	66	848	938
8	11	544	839
1	11	383	839
2	73	774	447

Protection from Envy. Write this square on parchment. On the back, write the name or names of the people who are jealous of your accomplishments. Then burn the square in the flame of a candle. You will be free of the evil energies of envious people.

POWER SQUARES first appeared in written form in a long lost XVIII century ancient grimore. Before that, they were handed down in occult circles only to the initiated. They have been used by many practitioners with great success.

Runes Symbols 1/2

Algiz. Ward off evil. Protection.	**Anzuz.** Communication. True vision.	**Berkano.** Birth. Fertility. New beginnings. Growth.	**Dagaz.** Awakening. Dawn. Breakthrough.	**Ehwaz.** Change. Trust. Loyalty. Teamwork.	**Eihwas.** Transition. Transformation. Passing through a gate.
Fehu. Wealth. Good Luck. Creation. Fertility.	**Gebo.** Contracts. Gifts. Exchanges. Partnerships.	**Hagalaz.** Uncontrolled Forces.	**Ingwas.** Gestation. Internal growth. Male fertility.	**Isa.** Challenge. Psychological blocks to be removed.	**Jera.** Peace. Prosperity. Fruitful Harvest.
Kenaz. Revelation. Vision.	**Laguz.** Power of Renewal. Dreams.	**Mannaz.** Friends & enemies. Social order.	**Nauthiz.** Endurance. Survival.	**Othala.** Heritage. Land of birth. Homeland.	**Perthro.** Occult abilities. Secrets to be revealed.
Raidho. Evolution. Journey. Travel.	**Sowilo.** Success. Goals. Honors and recognition.	**Thurisaz.** Reactive force. Defense.	**Tiwas.** Leadership. Justice. Authority.	**Uruz.** Untamed potential. Physical Strength.	**Wunjo.** Joy. Contentment. Pleasure.

The above runes have been used for magical or divinatory purposes from A.D. 150 in the Scandinavian area. They can also be used for meditation or carved/painted in amulets and talismans.

Rune Numbers 2/2

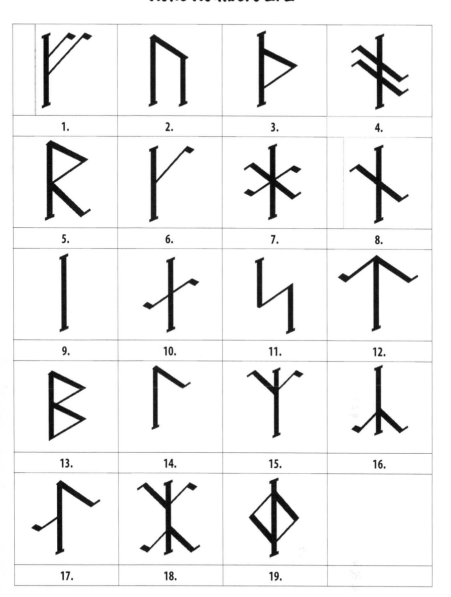

Rune Numbers. These numbers come from the Runic Calendar used on the Nordic countries until the 19th century. This calendar is based on the Metonic cycle correlating the Sun and the Moon. This calendar was marked to observe the full moon, the new moon, and special days like solstices, equinoxes, holidays, and feasts. You can use these numbers on your DIY shields and seals.

Jewish Amulets 1/2

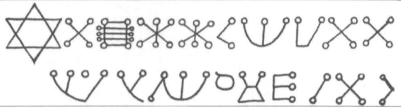

For Grace And Favor. "Write upon deer-skin: 'By Thy universal name of grace and favor yhvh, set Thy grace yhvh upon N, son of N, as it rested upon Joseph, the righteous one, as it is said, "And the Lord was with Joseph, and showed kindness unto him, and gave him favor" in the sight of all those who beheld him [Gen. 39:21]. In the name of Michael, Gabriel, Raphael, Uriel, Kabshiel, Yah (repeated eight times), Ehyeh, Ahah (four times), Yehu (nine times)'"

To safeguard a man against all weapons.

These medieval amulets were very popular and contained the most powerful elements of Jewish magic. They were prepared by experts to meet particular needs. Many of them cited Biblical quotations.

Jewish Amulets 2/2

The Qabbalistic, and Magic Alphabets. Medieval philosophers used these alphabets to conceal their doctrines and tenets from the profane. Its figures are derived from the constellations. Advanced students of occult philosophy will come upon many valuable documents in which these figures are used. Under each letter of the first alphabet above is its equivalent in English. Above each letter of the other three alphabets is its Hebrew letter equivalent.

Chinese, Japanese, and Tibetan Talismans

 **Coins.** Chinese. Used to bring in wealth, positive energies, and prosperity.	 **Shield.** Bronze Age. Protection in all aspects of daily life.	 **Tho.** Chinese. Longevity.
 **Hematite.** Upper Congo. Protection against disease.	 **Blue Flint.** Egyptian. To secure and maintain good health.	 **Arrow Head.** Japanese. Protection from disease and Evil Eye.
 **Buddha.** Tibetan. Happiness, prosperity, knowledge, and deliverance from enemies.	 **Tau Cross.** Associated with many beliefs. Authority. Power. Protection.	 **Turtle.** China, Japan & India. To repel black magic and as a symbol of longevity.
 **The Serpent.** Japanese. Longevity. Health. Vitality.	 **Sun Talisman.** India. New beginnings. Unending time.	 **Pa-kwa.** Chinese. Long life under auspicious circumstances.

Chinese, Japanese, Hindu, and Tibetan Talismans

Buddah's Footprints. Tibetan. For wisdom and enlightment.

Seven Knotted Bamboo. Hindu. Wisdom, perseverance, and power.

Ganesa. Hindu. The remover of obstacles.

Lucky Diagram. Tibetan. Longevity.

Lotus. Hindu. Good luck, good fortune, and beauty.

The Conch Shell. Hindu. The bringer of wealth, oratory teacher, and aid in any type of learning.

The Money Sword. Chinese. Suspended from right to left above the head of the bed. All powerful protection against ill-luck, and evil spirits. Also attracts cash.

The Keys of the Granary. Japanese. Worn for love, wealth, and happiness.

The Fish. Hindu. For fertility and to increase riches.

Hanuman. Hindu. Medicine, magic, and to defeat enemies.

The Three Gems Talisman. For Endurance, courage, and obedience according to Buddhist Law.

Chinese, Japanese, Shinto, and Tibetan Talismans

The Thunderbolt of Indra. Tibet. Against demons and to bring fruitfulness.	**The Dragon.** Tibet. For Domestic Felicity.	**The Fan.** China. For power and authority.

The Silver Triangle. China. For protection against ghosts and goblins.	**The Torii.** Shinto. Rectitude, obedience, fidelity, and justice.	**The Mitsu-Domoe.** Japan. Protection from fire, flood, and theft.

Islamic Talismans

In the name of Allah, you shall have clear thoughts in a peaceful mind.	In the name of Allah, you shall be protected.	In the name of Allah you shall live in paradise.

In the name of Allah, you shall prosper and have good fortune.	In the name of Allah, all secrets on earth and heaven will be revealed to you.	In the name of Allah, you will receive mercy, compassion, and grace.

Voodoo Veves 1/2

Productivity. To accomplish all tasks.	**Come to Me.** To attract love, devotion from loved ones.	**Deliverance.** To get rid of any type of addictions.	**Insanity.** Place it on your foes clothes to cause confusion.

Pay me now. To collect any money or promises owed to the possessor.	**All Spirits.** Communicate safely with entities on the other side.	**Sexual Magnet.** Makes possessor's sexual vibration irresistible to others.	**Demolisher.** Quickly stops plots or tricks planned against the possessor.

Exorciser. Protection against evil spirits and demons.	**Job Hunting.** Use it before, during, and after a job interview.	**Bridal Veil.** Entice suitors to propose marriage.	**Tip the Scales.** Make others grant you favors.

Casino. Use this before, during, and after playing games of chance.	**Win in court.** Use this before, during, and after court or legal cases.	**Sensual Wanga.** Arouses women's desire and men's potency in sexual encounters.	**Back to Zero.** Helps to remove, solve, or receive pardon from consequences of past mistakes.

Voodoo Veves 2/2

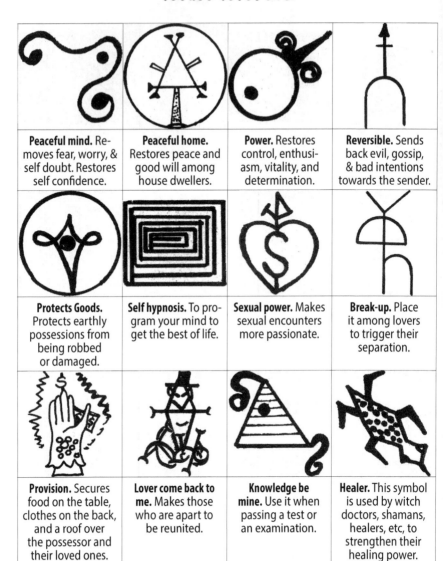

Peaceful mind. Removes fear, worry, & self doubt. Restores self confidence.	**Peaceful home.** Restores peace and good will among house dwellers.	**Power.** Restores control, enthusiasm, vitality, and determination.	**Reversible.** Sends back evil, gossip, & bad intentions towards the sender.
Protects Goods. Protects earthly possessions from being robbed or damaged.	**Self hypnosis.** To program your mind to get the best of life.	**Sexual power.** Makes sexual encounters more passionate.	**Break-up.** Place it among lovers to trigger their separation.
Provision. Secures food on the table, clothes on the back, and a roof over the possessor and their loved ones.	**Lover come back to me.** Makes those who are apart to be reunited.	**Knowledge be mine.** Use it when passing a test or an examination.	**Healer.** This symbol is used by witch doctors, shamans, healers, etc, to strengthen their healing power.

Veves, how to use them. A veve is a religious symbol that represents a loa or deity during voodoo rituals. They represent astral forces and their energy is conjured during rituals so they descend to earth to listen to the practitioner's petitions during the ceremony. A veve is commonly drawn on the floor where the ceremony or ritual is going to take place. It can be drawn with any powder, usually a ground grain, such as corn, or wheat, mixed with bark, or brick powder, and even gun powder. It all depends on the practitioner's preferences. Veves can also be embroidered, or made into patchwork, carried on talismans, wall hangings, banners, etc, to draw a loa or deity's energies upon the user or habitants of the place where it is showcased.

Wiccan Symbols 1/4

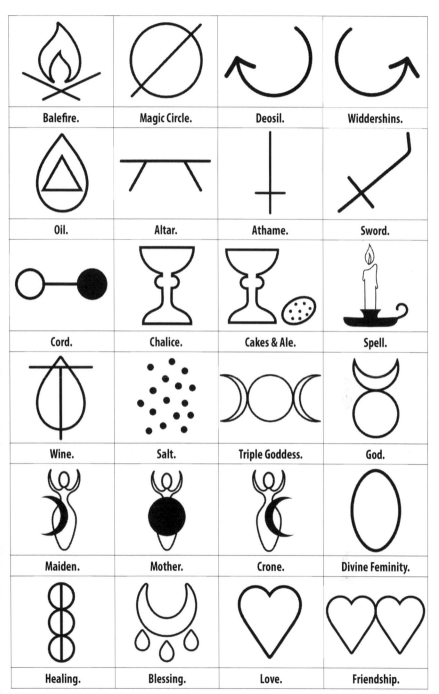

Wiccan Symbols 2/4

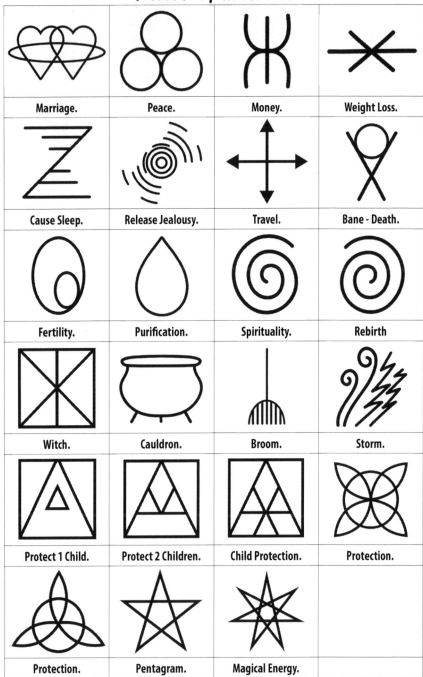

Wiccan Symbols 3/4

| Sunrise. | Sunset. | Moonrise. | Moonset. |

| Triple Goddess with Pentagram. | Pentagram with Elements. |

| Physical & Magical Strength. | Psychic Awareness. |

| Beltane. | Imbolc. | Lammas. | Litha. |

| Mabon. | Ostara. | Samhain. | Yule. |

Wiccan Symbols 4/4

Wheel of the Year. Candlemas. Spring Equinox. May Day. Summer Solstice. Lunghnasadh. Autumn Equinox. All Hallows Eve. Winter Solstice.

Miscellaneous 1/3

The Pythagoreans Signet Ring. For Good Health and for Healing.	**The Scorpion Talisman.** For curing diseases, specially those affecting the reproduction system.	**The Tetragramaton.** The supreme light for the practice of White Magic.
	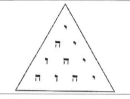	
The Supreme Definitionless Creator. To invoke God.	**The 72 powers of the Great Name of God.** To Invoke God with all His Great Names.	**The Trinity.** To invoke the Three Divine Generations.

The Crucified Rose. A rose rising from the cross, symbolizing unity and hope.	**The Rosicrucian Rose.** For Fecundity, purity, and spiritual enfoldment.	**The Tree of Alchemy.** With all 14 steps: Solution, Filtration, Evaporation, Distillation, Separation, Rectification, Calcination, Commixtion, Purification, Inhibition, Fermentation, Fixation, Multiplication, and Projection, or the process of turning the base Metals into gold.

Miscellaneous 2/3

Form of Bond of Spirits Given in 1573.

I, Pabiel, ministering Spirit and messenger of the presiding and ruling Spirit of Jupiter, appointed thereunto by the Creator of all things visible and invisible, do swear, promise, and plight my faith and troth unto thee in the presence and before the great יהוה and the whole company and host of Heaven, and by all the Holy Names of God do swear and bind myself unto thee by all the contents of God's Sacred Writ, by the Incarnation, Death, and Passion, by the Resurrection and glorious Ascension of JC, by all the holy Sacraments, by the Mercy of God, by the Glory of Joys of Heaven, by the forgiveness of sin and hope of eternal salvation, by the Great Day of Doom, by all Angels, Archangels, Seraphim, Cherubim, Dominations, Thrones, Principalities, Powers, and Virtues, and all the other blessed and glorious company of Heaven, by all the constellations of Heaven, and by all the several Powers and Virtues, above rehearsed, and by whatsoever else is holy or binding, do I swear, promise, and bow unto thee that I will appear, come, and haste unto thee and at all times and places and in all hours, days, and minutes, from this time forward unto thy life's end wheresoever thou shalt call me by my name or by my office, and I will come unto thee in what form thou shalt desire, either visibly or invisibly, and will answer all thy desires and give testimony thereof and let all the powers of Heaven witness it.

I have hereunto subscribed my hand and confirm my seal and character unto thee. Amen.

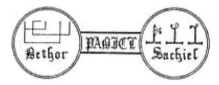

Form of Bond for the Invocation of Spirits. The above figure is a complete and faithful representation of a Magic Circle as designed by medieval conjurers for the invocation of spirits. The magician accompanied by his assistant takes his place at the point formed by the crossing of the central lines marked MAGISTER. The words in the the circle are the names of the invisible intelligences, and the small crosses mark points at which certain prayers and invocations are recited. The small circle outside is prepared for the spirit to be invoked, and while in use has the signature of the desired intelligence traced within the triangle.

Miscellaneous 3/3

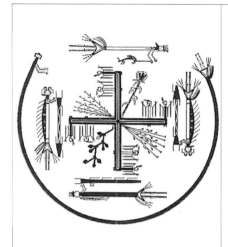

The Navajo Sand Painting. This drawing is prepared on the sand for the healing of disease. In the healing ceremony the patient is placed upon the drawing, which is made in a consecrated hogan, and all outsiders are excluded. When the ceremony is finished, the drawing is swept by the hand of the healer.

The Most Powerful Hand. Upon the twelve phalanges of the fingers, appear the images of the Apostles, each bearing its own appropriate symbol. On the second phalange of the thumb is Jesus Christ, and on the first phalange of the thumb is the Virgin Mary. Used for protection.

The Third Pythagorical Synod. A hermaphroditic figure represents the active, and passive principles of Nature, male, and female, harmoniously conjoined to symbolize the state of perfect equilibrium.

The Phoenix On Its Nest Of Flames. The Phoenix is the most celebrated of all the symbolic creatures fabricated by the ancient Mysteries for the purpose of concealing the great truths of esoteric philosophy. It represents rebirth, renewal. Construction upon the ashes. The relentless force of life.

DIY Magical Seals 1/3

You can make your very own magical seals. Here is how to do it.

First, create a phrase or word that represents what you want to use your seal for.

Use positive affirmative words in present time. For example, don't say "Pay my Debts". A better saying would be: "Be Debt Free", "Have Economic Freedom", or "Be Wealthy".

Let's work an example with this phrase: Own a House

Then use this table to get the numbers:

1	2	3	4	5	6	7	8	9
a	b	c	d	e	f	g	h	i
j	k	l	m	n	o	p	q	r
s	t	u	v	w	x	y	z	

O-w-n-a-H-o-u-s-e

6-5-5-1-8-6-3-1-5

Then delete repeated numbers:

6-5-1-8-3

The create the form of your first symbol:

1 2 3 / 4 5 6 / 7 8 9	. . . / . . . / . . .
Here, you can see the position of the numbers.	Here, you trace a line connecting the dots with the same order as your numbers: 6-5-1-8-3

DIY Magical Seals 2/3

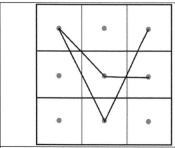
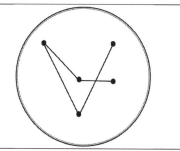

Here are the results: the dots connected with your numbers representing your wish. Are you feeling the energy yet?	Then, take the figure and draw it into a circle. Afterwards, you write around the circle whatever you want that will reinforce the energy of your wish.

Examples of what to write around the circle, inside and/or outside:

1. Initials of your name and/or initials of the name of the person your are casting the spell for. (See Jewish Amulets section for a very cool alphabet).

2. Your birthdate and/or their birthdate. (See Runes Section for number symbols)

3. Symbol of your zodiac sign and/or their zodiac sign. (See Zodiac section)

4. The date you created the seal, so you can see the progress of your petition.

5. Your favorite archangel, saint, deity or higher power to whom you're addressing this petition. (See section Shields of the Saints)

6. The symbol or drawing of an object that makes you feel strong, in command and powerful. It can be as simple as a pen, if you're a writer or as complicated as a tractor if you're a farmer. Up to you.

7. Coordinates of the location, or zip code where you are casting the spell to.

8. Anything else that works for you and will make this seal stronger.

Now follow instructions on consecrating your seal. (See how-to section at the beginning of the book).

Carry it with you or hang it in your favorite spot and don't fret. Be mindful that magic takes time. You have sown a seed on the spiritual plane and it will sprout and give fruits in its due time.

If your seal is for protection, carry it with you and touch it everytime you need to connect with its energy and fill you in with it.

In the next page, you will find two drawings you can copy to make your own magical seal. You can enlarge or reduce them to the size of your preference.

Blessed Be.

DIY Magical Seals 3/3

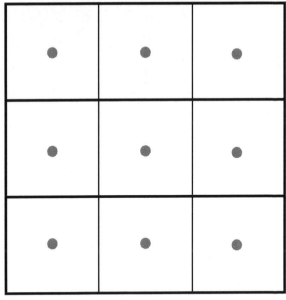

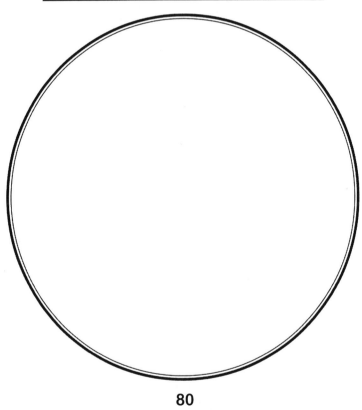

General Index

Symbols

1-19 Numbers, 63
1st Heaven, 12
2nd Heaven, 13
3rd Heaven, 13
4th Heaven, 12
5th Heaven, 13
6th Heaven, 13
7 African Powers, 10
7 Archangels, 11
7 Drops of Love, 11
7th Heaven, 13
7x7 Against All, 11

A

Achievement of Goals, 35
Adam & Eve, 11
Against demons, 68
Against Evil, 11, 48
Aid in any type of learning, 67
Air, 12, 49
All Hallows Eve, 74
All points protection and affirmation of power, 33
All secrets on earth and heaven will be revealed to you, 68
All Spirit, 69
Alms, 55
Altar, 71
Anael, 13
Anchor, 52, 57
Angel, 51
Angels, 12, 14
Appears as a woman, this spirit is the only one who, 31
Apply to affected areas to release a relentless healing power, 23
Aquarius, 13, 15, 16
Araboth, 13
Archangels, 34
Aries, 13, 15, 16
Arouses women's desire and men's potency in sexual encounters, 69
Arrow Head, 66
Arrows, 57
Ascendant, 16
Assistance in magical endeavors, 44
Astral travelling, 27
Astral travels, 31
Athame, 71
Attract-Attract, 9
Attract Customers, 11
Attracts cash, 67
Authority, 62, 66
Autumn, 12
Autumn Equinox, 74
Awakening, 62
Awarenes, 48

B

Baby Jesus, 53
Back to zero, 69
Balance of Justice, 11
Balefire, 71
Bane, 72
Banner with angel, 53
Bee, 54
Being wise with your time, 48
Bell, 55
Beltane, 73
Be Quiet, 9
Better Business, 11
Birth. Fertility, 62
Black, 17
Black Destroyer, 11
Black Madona of Czestochowa, 52
Blessed, 9
Blessing, 71
Blue, 17
Blue Flint, 66
Blue sash, 52
Book, 54
Bread, 54
Bread provision, 19
Breakthrough, 62
Break-up, 70
Bridal Veil, 10, 69
Bright Day, 17
Broken wheel, 54
Bronze Age, 66
Bronze crown, 52
Broom, 56, 72
Brown, 17
Buddah's Footprints, 67
Buddha, 66

C

Caffiel, 13
Cakes & Ale, 71
Camael, 13
Cancer, 12, 15, 16
Candlemas, 74
Cape, 56
Capricorn, 13, 15, 16
Carpenter's ruler, 56
Casino, 69
Cauldron, 72
Cause Sleep, 72

Caution, 48
Ceres, 16
Chalice, 55, 71
Challenge, 62
Change, 62
Change a man into a dog, 21
Charm and Enchantment, 10
Chasuble, 55
Cherub, 52
Child of Atocha, 11
Child Protection, 72
Children, 57
Chinese, 66, 67, 68
Chiron, 16
Ciborium, 54
Clarity, 48
Cleansing, 11
Club, 51
Coins, 51, 66
Column, 51
Comet, 16
Come to Me, 9, 10, 69
Come To Me, 11
Communicates with All, 38
Communication, 62
Communion, 54
Congo, 66
Conjuction, 16
Conjuration of Power, 35
Conqueror, 11
Constellations, 15
Contentment, 17, 62
Contracts, 62
Control, 11
Controls Evil, 39
Cord, 71
Couple love drawing, 19
Court or legal cases, 69

Coyote, 11
Creation, 60, 62
Crescent Moon, 52
Crisis, 33
Crone, 71
Crosier, 55
Cross, 55, 56
Cross and rose, 57
Crowned heart, 53
Crown of 12 stars, 53
Crown of thorns, 54
Crucified Rose, 75
Crucifix, 54
Cube, 49
Cushion, 52

D

Dawn, 62
Days, 12
Deacon's vestments, 55
Death, 72
Defense, 62
Deliverance, 69
Deliverance from enemies, 66
Deliverance from fear, 44
Demolisher, 69
Deosil, 71
Destroy Everything, 9
Destroys Evil, 37
Direct, 16
Discover Secrets, 35
Discover treasures, 35
Divine protection, 41
Divine Trinity, 11
Dog, 57
Don Juan Mr. Money, 11
Door, 54
Door opener without a key, 19

Double Good Luck, 9, 11
Dove, 56
Dragon, 53, 55, 68
Dragon in chains, 56
Dreams, 62

E

Eagle, 51
Earth, 12, 16, 22, 49
Earth Orb, 48
Egyptian, 66
Eight pointed star, 52
Elements, 12
Endows Virtue and Talent, 37
Endurance, 62
Enjoyment, 60
Essential nature, 60
Ether, 12, 49
Evil eye, 59, 66
Evolution, 62
Exchanges, 62
Exorciser, 69
Eyes, 56

F

Facilitates marriage proposals, and makes love flourish, and freely flow, 30
Faith, 17
Family love drawing, 19
Fan, 68
Fast Money, 9, 10, 11
Fertility, 17, 62, 72
Fire, 12, 22, 49
Fire divination, 19
Fish, 67
Fish provision, 19
Fleur de Lis, 52

Flowers, 53
For achieving victory in all endeavors under divine protection, 41
For a house to fall down, 19
For curing diseases, specially those affecting the reproduction system, 75
For divination of past and future, 19
For dizziness relief, 21
For Domestic Felicity, 68
For Endurance, courage, and obedience according to Buddhist Law, 67
For Fecundity, purity, and spiritual enfoldment, 75
For fertility and to increase riches, 67
For glass or mirror divination, 22
For Good Health and for Healing, 75
For good luck, good health, and wisdom, 59
For Grace And Favor, 64
For healing all leg and foot ailments, 58
For jewels to be found, 20
For job seekers, 42
For long life under auspicious circumstances, 66
For Love, 46
For Love Between A Man and His Wife, 46
For love, wealth, and happiness, 67
For magical protection, 59
For medical assistance in obtaining health in body, mind, and spirit, 40
Form for the Invocation of Spirits, 76

For power and authority, 68
For protection, 39, 47
For protection against ghosts and goblins, 68
For protection, and power, 34
For protection from all evil spirits, 58
For protection in quarrels, wars, disputes, and disagreements, 58
For quick answers, 50
For rubies to be found, 19
For sexual vibration to be irresistible to others, 69
For silver coins to be found, 22
For strength and power, 33
For the conjuration of celestial and infernal powers, 35
For the healing of disease, 77
For truce, reconciliation, and peace among parties, 59
Fortune, Lot of, 16
For wealth, and for vengeance endeavors, 40
For wealth and prosperity, 50
For wealth, honors, and good health endeavors, 40
For Whoever Wisheth For A Woman, 46
For wisdom and enlightment, 67
For wisdom, perseverance, and power, 67
Fox, 54
Friday, 13
Friends & enemies, 62
Friendship, 71

Fruitful Harvest, 62

G

Gabriel, 12
Games of chance, 42, 69
Ganesa, 67
Garlic, 11
Gemini, 13, 15, 16
Gestation, 62
Gifts, 62
Gives Good Fortune, 38
Gives Healing Powers, 37
Gives Knowledge, 38
Gives the love and complaisance of the entire female sex, 35
Goals, 62
God, 71
Good Luck, 17, 62
Good luck, good fortune, and beauty, 67
Good Luck & Protection, 11
Goodwill, 17
Green, 17
Growth, 62

H

Halo of stars, 53
Hand healing, 19
Hand holding candle, 52
Handkerchief, 53
Handkerchief with tears, 52
Hands praying, 52
Hands with rosary, 53
Hanuman, 67
Happiness, 66
Head in hands, 55
Healer, 70
Heal from curses, 20
Health & Vitality, 66

He arouses desire and passion between the couple, 32
Heart, 56, 57
Heart pierced with a sword, 52
He breaks up love in married or unmarried couples, 28
He brings back harmony in the house, 30
He brings in help from someone close, 31
He brings in wealth and prosperity, 31
He brings out hero traits to the bearer, 31
He can adjust time at will, 32
He can advise you of your enemies' desires, 28
He can be invoked only under the sign of Saggittarius to heal emotional wounds, and to strengthen relationships, 30
He can bring about anything to happen instantly, 29
He can bring about disaster, and death attached to storms at sea, 29
He can bring back the souls of the dead to answer questions, 28
He can bring destruction to or help you reconcile with enemies, 29
He can cause man or woman to show themselves naked, 29
He can change anyone into any shape without their knowledge, 28
He can change others into animals, 29
He can create anything you ask him for, 28
He can cure all illnesses with magic, 29
He can draw love from enemies, 31
He can either cause or cure diseases or maladies, 31
He can help the sorcerer to reconcile with enemies, 30
He can help you have an engaging conversation, 32
He can help you pass any exam in any subject, 32
He can help you when you need to find a lost treasure, a good job, a good friend, or a lucky number, 32
He can induce murder and death, 28
He can make men witty, 29
He can make petty disputes escalate into full blown wars, 29
He can modify time to suit the sorcerer's needs, 29
He can prevent a tree from producing fruit, 30
He can protect the sorcerer and destroy their enemies, 29
He can punish those who have wronged the sorcerer, 28
He can read past and present, 31
He can reveal souls of the dead who died in sin, 29
He can steal money, find stolen goods, and bring someone close to assist the sorcerer, 29
He can take away sight, hearing, or understanding from anyone, 29
He can teach you Arts and Sciences, 32
He can teach you philosophy, 28
He can turn wine into water, blood into wine, or metals into coins, 29
He casts away evil spirits or vindictive entities, 32
He converts metals into gold, 30
He draws success in business and financial matters, 31
He dresses in red, and can change the shape of others at will, 32
He enlightens in astrology issues, 30
He enlightens the mind of the bearer when he has to make a decision in a seemingly hopeless situation, 30
He foretells the future, 30
He gives you information of past, and future happenings, 32
He governs over 30 legions of Spirits, 28
He governs over thunder and lightning, and reveals other's secret thoughts, 28
He governs over war, 28
He governs over wind and water, 28
He grants favors in legal issues and court cases, 31
He grants invisibility, 28
He grants protection from

evildoers, 31
He grants protection from harm, envy, and hatred, 30
He grants the ability to use words in a clever and funny way with a sharper mind, 30
He grants the ability to use words with elegance and acuity, 31
He grants the sorcerer skilled hands, and sharpness of mind, 29
He grants the sorcerer the power to dominate and subjugate others, 28
He grants wisdom, and helps the bearer find stolen or hidden things, 31
He helps find lost or misplaced things, 32
He helps in astral travels, 31
He helps in decision making, 30
He helps recover from addictions, specially from alcohol, 30
He helps recover lost honors or possesions, 32
He helps recover lost things, 31
He helps the bearer gain control,, courage, 31
He helps the bearer get on top of arguments or quarrels, 32
He helps the bearer receive honors, 31
He helps the sorcerer know what others are thinking, 29
He helps the sorcerer to receive honors, recognition, and good social standing, 30
He helps the sorcerer to still his mind, and get rid of fear, 31
He helps the sorcerer to uncover the unknown, 30
He helps to dominate others, 32
He helps uncover hidden treasures, 30
He imparts cure for all maladies, and diseases, 30
He inflames passions, love, and lust, 29
He is a poet that will obey all your requests, 32
He is promoter of love and good will, 30
He is sweet, and speaks with the voice of a child, 32
He is the protector of the military, 29
Helm, 52
He makes foes or enemies switch positions in favor of the bearer, and gain a higher, more respected position, 32
He makes polarizing emotions (love or hate) flow into an environment, 31
Hematite, 66
He prevents wounds from healing, 29
He prevents wounds from healing, 28
He procures knowledge in the magical use of stones, herbs, and astrology, 31
He promotes wealth and good fortune, 30
He promotes wealth, and wisdom, 31
He protects from nightmares & restlessness. Induces revelatory dreams, 24
He protects from slander and persecution, 32
He protects from storms, hurricanes, earthquakes, or tornadoes, 24
He protects the sorcerer, and can destroy one's foes, 28
He reads past and future, 29
He reveals the future, 30
He reveals the future through visions and dreams, 30
Heritage, 62
He rules over plants and stones, 28
He sinks ships, and can cause death by drowning, 28
He strengthens courage, 30
He strengthens loyalty and fidelity, 32
He takes the shape of a Raven, 32
He takes the shape of a wolf, 32
He teaches knowledge on stones, and plants, as well as logic, 31
He teaches literature, 31
He teaches logic and philosophy, 30
He teaches sciences, arts, and languages, 31
He will bring together in love any couple, 32
He will create friendship,

love, and self esteem, 32
He will help the sorcerer in all job related endeavors, 30
He will reel into submission a person posed against the sorcerer, 29
He will reveal the identity of other witches and sorcerers to the possessor, 29
He will send someone close to assist in a secret endeavor, 30
He will steal money on behalf of the sorcerer, 29
Hex Breaker, 11
Hex breaking, 48
Hind, 55
Hindu, 67
Holy Death, 9, 10, 11, 48
Holy Spirit, 52
Holy water sprinkler, 56
Homeland, 62
Honey of Love, 11
Honors, 62
Hourglass, 48
Hummingbird, 9, 10

I

I Can and You Can't, 11
IHS symbol, 54
I'll Succeed, 9
Imbolc, 73
Immaculare Heart of Mary, 52
Improve Business, 9, 10
Inconjunt, 16
Initiation ceremonies and rituals, 59
Insanity, 69
Internal growth, 62
Invisibility, 25, 28, 36
Islamic, 68
Ivory carving, 53

J

Japanese, 66, 67, 68
Jewelled crown with hearts, 52
Job Hunting, 69
Job interview, 69
Journey, 62
Joy, 62
Judas Iscariot, 51
June, 16
Jupiter, 13, 16, 18, 23
Justice, 48, 62
Just Judge, 11

K

Keep Away Evil, 17
Ketu, 16
Keys, 51, 55
Keys of the Granary, 67
Knife, 51
knowledge, 19, 66
Knowledge be mine, 70
kundalini, 60

L

Lamb, 54, 56
Lammas, 73
Lamp, 48
Lance, 51
Land of birth, 62
Law on my Side, 9
Leadership, 62
Leo, 12, 15, 16
Libra, 13, 15, 16
Lilith, 16
Lion, 55, 56
Litha, 73
longevity, 66, 67
Lotus, 67
Love, 71
Love Drawing, 11
Lover come back to me, 70
Loyalty, 62
Lucky Diagram, 67
Lucky Stars, 17
Lunghnasadh, 74

M

Mabon, 73
Macaw Bird, 10
Machen, 12
Machon, 13
Magical Energy, 72
Magic Alphabet, 65
Magic Circle, 71
Magic drawing, 19
Maiden, 71
Makes sexual encounters more passionate, 70
Makes those who are apart to be reunited, 70
Make women quarrel, 21
Male fertility, 62
Mantle, 53
Marriage, 72
Mars, 13, 16, 18, 23
Marta Dominadora, 9
Master of all knowledge in regards to plants, stones, and the stars, 32
Master of languages, 29
Master of Mathematics, 27
Master of science and occult wisdom, 28
Master of the waters, 29
Master the art of rhetoric, 32

May Day, 74
Meat provision, 19
Medicine, magic,, 67
Men's potency, 69
Mercury, 13, 16, 18, 24
Metal, 22
Michaiel, 12
Midheaven, 16
Mitsu-Domoe, 68
Monday, 12
Money, 72
Money Sword, 67
Monstrance, 55
Moon, 12, 16, 18, 24
Most Powerful Hand, 11, 77
Mother, 71

N

Nailed hands, 57
Nails, 56
Navajo Sand Painting, 77
Neptune, 16
New beginnings, 62, 66
Numbers 1-19, 63

O

Occult abilities, 62
Oil, 71
Olive branch, 52
Opens even the strongest of doors or locks, 24
Opens locks, 36
Ophiuchus, 16
Opportunity is Knocking, 9
Orange, 17
oratory teacher, 67
Orb of the Earth, 53
Organ, 54
Ostara, 73

Our Lady of Aparecida, 52
Our Lady of Camarin, 52
Our Lady of Candelaria, 52
Our Lady of Charity, 52
Our Lady of Chiquinquirá, 53
Our Lady of Copacabana, 52
Our Lady of Cotoca, 52
Our Lady of Fátima, 52
Our Lady of Good Counsel, 52
Our Lady of Guadalupe, 52
Our Lady of Humility, 52
Our Lady of Itatí, 52
Our Lady of Lebanon, 52
Our Lady of Lourdes, 52
Our Lady of Luján, 52
Our Lady of Mount Carmel, 53
Our Lady of Navigators, 52
Our Lady of Peace, 52
Our Lady of Peace and Good Voyage, 52
Our Lady of Peñafrancia, 53
Our Lady of Piat, 53
Our Lady of San Juan de los Lagos, 53
Our Lady of Sorrows, 53
Our Lady of the Garden Enclosed, 52
Our Lady of the Most Holy Rosary, Queen of, the Caracol, 53
Our Lady of the Rosary, 53
Our Lady of the Visitation of Guibang, 53
Our Lady of Vendôme, 53
Our Mother of Sheshan, 53
Owl, 48
Ox, 56, 57

P

Pa-kwa, 66
Pallas, 16
Palm, 57
Palm divination and reading, 19
Partnerships, 62
Passing through a gate, 62
Patchouli, 9, 11
Pay me now, 69
Pay Me Now, 9
Peace, 17, 62, 72
Peaceful home, 70
Peaceful mind, 70
Pen, 54, 55
Pentagram, 72, 73
Perfect equilibrium, 77
Personal talisman, 59
Physical & Magical Strength, 73
Physical Strength, 62
Pisces, 13, 15, 16
Planet, 12
Planets, 14
Pleasure, 62
Pluto, 16
Power, 48, 66, 70
Power of Renewal, 62
Power of Truth, 35
Productivity, 69
Promotes good, long lasting friendships, 26
Proserpine, 16
Prosperity, 17, 62, 66
Protect 1 Child, 72
Protect 2 Children, 72
Protect from enemies, 40
Protection, 9, 48, 66, 72
Protection against disease, 66

Protection against envy and the evil eye, 59
Protection against evil spirits, and demons, 69
Protection against ill-luck, and evil spirits, 67
Protection during travels, 50
Protection for home and possesions, 25
Protection from a violent death, 42
Protection from being bitten by poisonous creatures, 33
Protection from black magic, 44
Protection from danger, 23
Protection from danger and firearms, making the bearer strong as steel, 41
Protection from danger of any type, and deceitful attacks, 24
Protection from demons, 59
Protection from disease and Evil Eye, 66
Protection from enemies, 33
Protection from Envy, 9, 10, 11
Protection from evil spirits and evil doers, 25
Protection from evil spirits that my linger around, 23
Protection from fire, flood, and theft, 68
Protection from foot trouble, 58
Protection from harm, and to make enemies weapons turn on themselves, 23
Protection from harm to the possessor and to his or her space, 42
Protection from injuries intended to harm body or soul, 24
Protection from poverty, 23
Protection in all aspects of daily life, 66
Protection in the afterlife, 33
Protects earthly possessions from being robbed or damaged, 70
Protects from Accidents, 36
Protects from Animals, 38
Protects Goods, 70
Protects the Traveler, 36
Provision, 19, 70
Psychic Awareness, 73
Psychological blocks to be removed, 62
Pulpit, 57
Purification, 72
Purple, 17
Purse, 56
Pythagoreans Signet Ring, 75

Q

Qabbalistic Alphabet, 65
Quadrature, 16
Queen of Heaven, 53

R

Rahu, 16
Rain, 17
Raindrops, 53
Raphael, 13
Raquie, 13
Raven, 54

Rays of light, 52
Reactive force, 62
Reads Other's Thoughts, 37
Rebirth, renewal, 77
Recognition, 62
Rectitude, obedience, fidelity, and justice, 68
Red, 17
Redemption and Regeneration, 17
Release Jealousy, 72
Relief from body pains, 20
Remover of obstacles, 67
Removes fear, worry, self doubt, 70
Removes obstacles, 24
Repels Evil Spirits, 39
Restless, 9, 11
Restores control, enthusiasm, vitality, and determination, 70
Restores peace and good will among house dwellers, 70
Restores self confidence, 70
Resurrection, 33
Retrograde, 16
Revelation, 62
Reversible, 9, 11, 70
Road Opener, 9, 11
Rosa Mystica, 53
Rosary, 55
Rose, 53
Rosicrucian Rose, 75
Rue, 9

S

Sachiel, 13
Sacred Heart of Jesus, 50
Sagittarius, 13, 15, 16
Sagun, 13

Saint Acathius, 54
Saint Agatha, 54
Saint Agnes, 54
Saint Ambrose, 54
Saint Andrew, 51
Saint Anne,, Grandmother of Jesus, 54
Saint Anthony, 50
Saint Anthony of Padua, 54
Saint Augustine of Hippo, 54
Saint Barbara, 54
Saint Bartholomew, 51
Saint Basil, 50
Saint Benedict, 9, 54
Saint Bernardine of Siena, 54
Saint Bernard of Clairvaux, 54
Saint Blaise, 54
Saint Bonaventure, 54
Saint Boniface, 54
Saint Bridget of Sweden, 54
Saint Catherine, 54
Saint Catherine of Ricci, 54
Saint Catherine of Siena, 54
Saint Cecilia, 54
Saint Charles Borromeo, 54
Saint Christopher, 55
Saint Chrysotom, 56
Saint Clare of Assisi, 55
Saint Cosmas & Damian, 55
Saint Cyprian, 10
Saint Cyriacus, 55
Saint Cyril, 50
Saint Denis, 55
Saint Dominic, 55
Saint Elizabeth of Hungary, 55
Saint Erasmus, 55
Saint Eustace, 55

Saint Expedite, 50
Saint Francis of Assisi, 55
Saint Francis Xavier, 55
Saint Genevieve, 55
Saint George, 55
Saint Gertrude, 55
Saint Giles, 55
Saint Gregory I The Great, 55
Saint Helena, 55
Saint Ignatius of Loyola, 55
Saint Isadore, 55
Saint James The Great, 51
Saint James The Just, 51
Saint Jerome, 55
Saint John, 51
Saint John Berchmans, 56
Saint John of God, 56
Saint John The Baptist, 56
Saint Joseph, 56
Saint Jude, 9, 11, 51
Saint Justin Martyr, 56
Saint Lawrence, 56
Saint Leander of Seville, 56
Saint Liborius, 56
Saint Louis IX of France, 56
Saint, Lucy, 56
Saint Luke, 56
Saint Margaret, 56
Saint Marie Magdalene, 50
Saint Marilda, 56
Saint Mark, 56
Saint Martha, 56
Saint Martin Caballero, 56
Saint Martin of Porres, 56
Saint Mary, 50
Saint Matthew, 51
Saint Maurus, 56
Saint Michael, 50, 56
Saint Monica, 57

Saint Nicholas, 57
Saint Pantaleon, 57
Saint Patrick, 57
Saint Paul, 57
Saint Peter, 50, 51
Saint Phillip, 51
Saint Rita of Cascia, 57
Saint Roch, 57
Saint Rose of Lima, 57
Saint Sebastian, 57
Saint Simon, 51
Saint Teresa of Avila, 57
Saint Therese of Lisieux, 57
Saint Thomas, 51
Saint Thomas Aquinas, 57
Saint Vincent de Paul, 57
Saint Vincent Ferrer, 57
Saint Vitus, 57
Salt, 71
Samhain, 73
Sanctum sanctorum, 52
Saturday, 13
Saturn, 13, 16, 18, 25
Saw, 51
Scale, 48, 56
Scapular, 53
Scepter, 53
Scimitar, 56
Scorpio, 13, 15, 16
Scorpion Talisman, 75
Scroll, 57
Scythe, 48
Seasons, 12
Secrets to be revealed, 62
Secret thoughts, 28
Secures food on the table, clothes on the back, and a roof, 70
Selene, 16
Self hypnosis, 70

Self-realization, 60
Sends back evil, gossip, & bad intentions towards the sender, 70
Sensual Wanga, 69
Serpent, 66
Seven Knotted Bamboo, 67
Sextile, 16
Sexual encounters, 69
Sexual Magnet, 69
Sexual power, 70
Shamain, 12
Shamans, 70
Shamrock, 57
Shell, 54
She procures love of women, both young and old, 31
Shield, 66
Shinto, 68
Silver Triangle, 68
Sliver of moon, 53
Social order, 62
Spell, 71
Spellcasting on a man, 21
Spirituality, 72
Spiritual world, 34
Spring, 12
Spring Equinox, 74
Square ruler, 51
Stag, 55
Steady Job, 9, 10
Sticky-Sticky, 9
Stigmata, 54
Storm, 72
Straw basket, 52
Stuck-on-Me, 10
Success, 17, 48, 62
Summer, 12
Summer Solstice, 74
Sun, 12, 16, 17, 18, 25, 33
Sunday, 12
Sun Talisman, 66
Supreme Definitionless Creator, 75
Survival, 62
Swirls, 53
Sword, 51, 71

T

Taper, 54
Tau Cross, 66
Taurus, 13, 15, 16
Teacher of art, geometry, history, and literature, 27
Teacher of liberal sciences, 29
Teacher of philosophy and sciences, 31
Teamwork, 62
Tears, 57
Tetragramaton, 75
The 72 powers of the Great Name of God, 75
The bringer of wealth, 67
The Phoenix, 77
The relentless force of life, 33
Third Pythagorical Synod, 77
Tho, 66
Thorn, 57
Three Gems Talisman, 67
Thunderbolt of Indra, 68
Thunder drawing, 19
Thursday, 13
Thwart a sorcerer's power, 21
Tibetan, 66, 67, 68
Tied-On-To-Me, 9, 10
Tip the Scales, 69
To accomplish all tasks, 69
To achieve higher positions,, receive praise, and get help from friends, even foes, 30
To achieve power in any specific field, 42
To achieve success in a speedy way, 50
To arouse in him/her great passion and strong desire, 26
To ask questions, get answers, 27
To assure the possessor of wealth, prosperity, and all things related to earthly possesions, such as inheritances, treasures, and so forth, 47
To assure wealth, 43
To attain and preserve good health, 59
To attract all the good things in life, 41
To attract and hold on to love, 50
To attract favorable vibrations, 43
To attract friendship and power over others, 40
To attract love, devotion from loved ones, 69
To attract riches, honors, and peace of mind, 23
To attract success, honor, and respect from others, 40
To attract wealth, and prosperity in business, 23
To be awaken at the time this person is receptive to your words, 61
To be bestowed with admiration, great respect, and love, 26

To be protected from evil spirits or entities while spell casting or performing magical rituals, 61
To be released from prisons real or of their own making, 25
To be rid of sickness and maladies, 50
To bewitch a beast, 21
To bless beginnings, 33
To bring back someone who strayed, 27
To bring confusion to known enemies, 23
To bring down mighty people to their knees, 27
To bring fruitfulness, 68
To bring in all types of blessings, 33
To bring in armed allies, 22
To bring in front of the possessor treasures hidden nearby, 43
To bring in good news, and to control others, 25
To bring in happiness, and good luck, 33
To bring in help from the Spirits in cases when fast solutions are needed, 44
To bring in joy and good health, 33
To bring in peace to a person or place, 44
To bring in rain, 20
To bring in revelatory dreams, 34
To bring in snow, 19
To bring in vigor, and renewal of youth, 33
To bring in wealth, positive energies, and prosperity, 66
To bring life back to a situation, 33
To bring out innermost thoughts of others, 27
To bring spirits of the dead to answer questions, 27
To call upon the spirits, 34
To cause confusion, 69
To cause destruction by fire, 27
To cause financial and personal destruction to an enemy, 27
To change a man into an ass, 21
To change base metals into precious metals like silver and gold, 61
To collect any, money or promises owed to the possessor, 69
To communicate safely with entities on the other side, 69
To communicate with animals, 27
To communicate with God, 33
To compel the spirits to do his bidding, 47
To connect with the spiritual world, 34
To conquer all obstacles, 50
To contact departed souls, 40
To control a situation, 58
To create chimeras to influence others' minds, 27
To create favorable conditions for the petition of the possessor, 34
To creates noise to cause chaos and confusion among foes, 27
To defeat enemies, 67
To diffuse negative influences, 43
To direct a spell unto a head, 21
To dispose of everything negative, 34
To dominate and mesmerize others, 41
To draw blessings and success in business, family, and personal affairs, 42
To draw glory, riches, and social standing, 25
To draw good fortune, good health, and great success in all endeavors, 41
To draw great success, 42
To draw honor, wealth, and to obtain promotions, 42
To draw light from darkness, 34
To draw lucky numbers, 43
To draw mighty power, dominance, & strength, 44
To draw mystical powers and divine guidance, 40
To draw out earthly treasures, 40
To draw popularity, influence, dominance, 42
To draw success in business and money matters, 40
To draw support from deities in all endeavors, 41
To enable the possessors to recover from the ruins of cities, buildings, and the bottom of wells, 47
To enjoy a full and loving relationship with people surrounding the pos-

sessor, 43
To enjoy human pleasures, and long lasting unions, 33
To entice suitors to propose marriage, 69
To exert revenge on foes and enemies, 27
To find a good friend, 32
To find a good job, 32
To find a lost treasure, 32
To find a lucky number, 32
To find hard to come by answers, 27
To find lost things,, 27
To forsee the future, 31
To free oneself from limitations, 33
To gain and retain wealth and honors, 23
To gain other's respect and admiration, 20
To gain personal magnetism, 24
To gain respect of a judge, 21
To Gain the Love of All Living, 45
To gain the upper hand with competitors or adversaries, 25
To gain wisdom, protection, and divine guidance in all matters, 41
To get illumination from the goddess or female energy, 33
To get rid of any type of addictions, 69
To get vindication, even victory, in a confrontation of any kind, 23
To govern over demons, 23
To guarantee enthusiasm, ambition, and great courage in physical matters, 23
To guarantee good luck, 50
To guarantee love and fertility, 34
To guarantee that all basic needs are covered every day, 58
To guarantee visions, 23
To have a full, long, and happy life, 43
To have all basic needs covered, 42
To have revelatory dreams, and to have questions answered while being asleep, 58
To have secrets revealed to you during your dreams, 44
To have wine supply, 20
To have your questions answered during dreams, or in daylight visions, 43
To help you know innermost thoughts of others, 27
To humble those who oppose the bearer's wishes or commands, 25
To increase the faith of the possessor, 58
To invoke God, 75
To Invoke God with all His Great Names, 75
To invoke the Three Divine Generations, 75
To keep peace in love or friendship alliances, 43
To learn Machiavellian maneuvers, 27
To locate a lost object, 43
To locate lost or stolen objects, 44
To locate lost treasures, 40
To look older and confuse others, 19
To look younger, 21
To loosen chains and blinds, 34
To make a foe be possessed by demons, 25
To make all desires come to pass, 39
To make any person come to him or her even against their will, 26
To make foes or friends show their true colors and innermost thoughts, 25
To make long lasting friendships, 31
To make one's wishes or requests come to reality, 44
To make others do your bidding, 40
To make others grant you favors, 69
To make others listen, and fear the words of the bearer, 25
To make others love you more, 20
To make other submissive to one's wishes, 25
To make relationships and businesses live long, happy lives, 58
To make the bearer strong as steel, 41
To make wishes come true, 25
To make wishes come true, 40
To master alchemy and

chemistry, 43
To master arts and occult knowledge, 40
To mesmerize someone to obtain their secret knowledge, 40
Tongs, 54
To open prison's gates, 22
To overcome, dominate, & protect from enemies, 40
To overcome lost causes and insurmountable stakes, 24
To pass a test or an examination, 70
To prevent a person from straying away, 61
To program your mind to get the best of life, 70
To promote beautiful, restoring rain, 24
To promote wisdom, a clear mind, and a bright disposition, 44
To protect all property, 47
To protect places from collapsing, 20
To protect the heart from negative emotions, 33
To protect women and children especially during pregnancy, 58
To protect your secrets from being revealed to others, 44
To quickly find a job, 50
To raise quarrels, 19
To reach heaven on earth, 33
To reach hidden thoughts, and to gain knowledge of hidden things, 24
To receive all heart's wishes in matters of love, 26
To receive help in astral travelling, 27
To receive knowledge on herbs, stones, astrology, and mathematics, 27
To receive prompt help when needed, 33
To receive the most divine of all blessings from the All Mighty, 41
To remove, solve, or receive pardon from consequences of past mistakes, 69
To repel black magic, 66
To restore, and to preserve good health, 50
To restore one's good health, 41
To reveal secrets, 27
To revert a magic spell, 21
Torii, 68
To rise above obstacles, even dead, 33
Torrent, 55
To safeguard a man against all weapons, 64
To secure and maintain good health, 66
To settle disputes, 42
To sharpen literary skills, 24
To silence gossip, slander, and evil doers, 59
To smite an enemy, 45
To stop plots or tricks planned against the possessor, 69
To strengthen your magical powers while casting any type of spell, 61
To strengthen healing power, 70
To strengthen one's faith, influence others, 41
To surround the possessor with love, 43
To tell apart false friends, 21
To transform people into birds, 27
To travel to any place in short time, 25
To trigger separation, 70
To uncover love secrets, 21
To uncover plots against the carrier, 27
To unearth precious metals from the earth, sunken ships from the water, or hidden treasures in abandoned places, 43
To unearth treasures, 43
To unveil mysteries from other planes, 27
Tower, 54
To win in legal and court cases, 42
To wreak vengeance upon an enemy, 45
Transformation, 62
Transforms water into wine, and all metals into gold, 28
Transition, 62
Transverse cross, 51
Travel, 62, 72
Tree of Alchemy, 75
Trine, 16
Trinity, 75
Triple Goddess, 71, 73
Triple Good Luck, 10, 11
True vision, 62
Trust, 62
Tuesday, 13
Turning the base Metals into gold, 75
Turtle, 66

Two crowns, 53

U

Unblocking, 9, 10
Unblocks roads, opens doors of any kind, 24
Uncontrolled Forces, 62
Uncover someone's riches, 20
Unending time, 66
unity and hope, 75
Untamed potential, 62
Uranus, 16
Use it to draw discord among others, and to outlast enemies, 23

V

Veil, 52
vengeance, 40
Venus, 13, 16, 18, 26
Vertex, 16
Vesta, 16
Vial, 55
Virgen de los Remedios de Pampanga, 53
Virgen del Valle, 53
Virgen of Miracles, 53
Virgin of, Montserrat, 53
Virgin of, the Thirty Tree, 53
Virgin or Mercy, 53
Virgo, 13, 15, 16
Vision, 62

W

Ward off evil. Protection, 62
Water, 12, 22, 49
Wealth, 17, 62
Wealth & Prosperity, 11
Wednesday, 13
Weed of Love, 10
Weight Loss, 72
Wheel of Fortune, 17
Wheel of the Year, 74
White, 17
White Magic, 75
Widdershins, 71
Windlass, 55
Wine, 71
Win in court, 69
Win in Court, 9, 10, 11
Winter, 12
Winter Solstice, 74
Win the Female, 35
Wisdom, 48
Witch doctors, 70
Wolf, 55

Women's desire, 69
Wood, 22
Wound healing, 20

Y

Yellow, 17
Your foe will get their due for all harm inflicted upon your person or property, 61
You shall be protected, 68
You shall have clear thoughts in a peaceful mind, 68
You shall live in paradise, 68
You shall prosper and have good fortune, 68
You will be free of the evil energies of envious people, 61
You will receive mercy, compassion, and grace, 68
Yule, 73

Z

Zebul, 13
Zodiac, 12, 15

© All rights reserved. No part of this book may be reproduced in text or images by any means, without written permission.
© 1st Edition Calli Casa Editorial 2023
© Yhacar Trust, 2023

By VICTORIA REY
General Supervision: Bernabé Pérez.
www.2GoodLuck.com
Calli Casa Editorial
Lake Elsinore, CA 92530

Printed in Poland
by Amazon Fulfillment
Poland Sp. z o.o., Wrocław